The poems of Lord Herbert of Cherbury;

Herbert of Cherbury, Edward Herbert, Baron, 1583-1648, John Churton Collins

Nabu Public Domain Reprints:

You are holding a reproduction of an original work published before 1923 that is in the public domain in the United States of America, and possibly other countries. You may freely copy and distribute this work as no entity (individual or corporate) has a copyright on the body of the work. This book may contain prior copyright references, and library stamps (as most of these works were scanned from library copies). These have been scanned and retained as part of the historical artifact.

This book may have occasional imperfections such as missing or blurred pages, poor pictures, errant marks, etc. that were either part of the original artifact, or were introduced by the scanning process. We believe this work is culturally important, and despite the imperfections, have elected to bring it back into print as part of our continuing commitment to the preservation of printed works worldwide. We appreciate your understanding of the imperfections in the preservation process, and hope you enjoy this valuable book.

POEMS OF LORD HERBERT.

THE
POEMS OF LORD HERBERT
OF CHERBURY

EDITED

WITH AN INTRODUCTION

BY

JOHN CHURTON COLLINS

LONDON
CHATTO AND WINDUS, PICCADILLY
1881

LONDON
PRINTED BY STRANGEWAYS AND SONS, TOWER STREET,
UPPER ST. MARTIN'S LANE, W C

I INSCRIBE

THIS LITTLE VOLUME

TO MY FRIEND

WILLIAM BAPTISTE SCOONES,

AN

IMPERFECT EXPRESSION

OF

ESTEEM AND AFFECTION.

PREFACE.

WHETHER the Poems, which are here for the first time presented in a modern dress, be of intrinsic value the reader will soon determine for himself. I have at least brought Herbert before the Court; and I have, I hope, secured him a fair hearing. Henceforth he will not be condemned unheard.

With regard to the text, I have adhered with scrupulous fidelity to that of the original edition; and I have collated the only two copies to which I could obtain access—the copy in the British Museum, and the copy in the Bodleian Library at Oxford—without, however, discovering any variety of readings. My principal difficulty has been with the punctuation, on which, of course, the sense of passages frequently depends; and for this I have often had no guidance *from the original, which teems with palpable errors. The spelling has also been carefully revised, and though it has been for the most part modernised, I have thought it well to retain, in some cases, the older forms, so as to preserve the flavour of archaism. Obvious misprints have been silently corrected. In two passages only I have ventured to alter the text, and they both occur in 'The Idea.' In the seventh line the original reads 'bear,' which, as it makes no sense, and breaks the rhyme, I alter into 'bar.' Again, in the last line, 'whence' is substituted for 'when.' And for this reason. Herbert is alluding to the Platonic doctrine of ideas, and it is much more natural to suppose that he would speak of an idea* whence *the form began than of an idea* when *the form began. Though he is mistaken in supposing that the Platonic ideas admit of application to particular individuals, he was evidently acquainted with the 'Timæus' and with the 'Republic.'*

J. CHURTON COLLINS.

5 King's Bench Walk, Temple.

CONTENTS.

	PAGE
INTRODUCTION	XV
ORIGINAL TITLE	XXXV
ORIGINAL PREFACE	XXXVII
TO HIS WATCH WHEN HE COULD NOT SLEEP	1
DITTY	2
A DESCRIPTION	3
TO HER FACE	6
TO HER BODY	7
TO HER MIND	8
UPON COMBING HER HAIR	10
DITTY IN IMITATION OF THE SPANISH ENTRE TANTOQUE EL'AVRIL	12
THE STATE PROGRESS OF ILL	14
SATYRA SECUNDA OF TRAVELLERS FROM PARIS	20
'I MUST DEPART, BUT LIKE TO HIS LAST BREATH'	24
MADRIGAL	25
ANOTHER	27

Contents.

	PAGE
TO HIS FRIEND BEN JOHNSON, OF HIS HORACE MADE ENGLISH	28
EPITAPH CÆCIL BOULFER QUÆ POST LANGUESCENTEM MORBUM NON SINE INQUIETUDINE SPIRITUS, &C. CONSCIENTIÆ OBIIT	29
EPITAPH GULI. HERBERT DE SWANSEY QUI SINE PROLE OBIIT, AUG. 1609	31
IN A GLASS WINDOW FOR INCONSTANCY	32
ELEGY FOR THE PRINCE	33
EPITAPH OF KING JAMES	36
A VISION A LADY COMBING HER HAIR	37
TEARS FLOW NO MORE	39
DITTY TO THE TUNE OF 'A CHE EL QUANTO MIO' OF PESARINO	40
DITTY	41
EPITAPH OF A STINKING POET	43
A DITTY TO THE TUNE OF 'COSE FERITE,' MADE BY LORENZO ALLEGRE TO ONE SLEEPING. (*To be sung*)	44
EPITAPH ON SIR EDWARD SACKVILLE'S CHILD, WHO DIED IN HIS BIRTH	45
KISSING	46
DITTY	47
ELEGY OVER A TOMB	49

Contents.

	PAGE
EPITAPH ON SIR FRANCIS VERE	51
TO MRS. DIANA CECYLL	52
TO HER EYES	54
TO HER HAIR	56
SONNET OF BLACK BEAUTY	58
ANOTHER SONNET TO BLACK IT SELF	59
THE FIRST MEETING	60
A MERRY RIME, SENT TO THE LADY WROTH UPON MY L OF PEMBROKE'S CHILD, BORN IN THE SPRING	64
THE THOUGHT	65
TO A LADY WHO DID SING EXCELLENTLY	67
MELANDER, SUPPOS'D TO LOVE SUSAN, BUT DID LOVE ANN	69
ECHO TO A ROCK	70
ECHO IN A CHURCH	72
TO HIS MISTRESS FOR HER TRUE PICTURE	74
EPITAPH ON SIR PHILIP SIDNEY, LYING IN ST. PAUL'S WITHOUT A MONUMENT, TO BE FASTENED UPON THE CHURCH DOOR	80
EPITAPH FOR HIMSELF	81
SONNET	82
TO THE C. OF D.	83
DITTY	84
ELEGY FOR DOCTOR DUNN	86

	PAGE
THE BROWN BEAUTY	90
AN ODE UPON A QUESTION MOVED WHETHER LOVE SHOULD CONTINUE FOR EVER	92
THE GREEN-SICKNESS BEAUTY	99
THE GREEN-SICKNESS BEAUTY	101
LA GRALLETTA GALLANTE; OR, THE SUN-BURN'D EXOTIQUE BEAUTY	102
PLATONICK LOVE	104
PLATONICK LOVE	106
THE IDEA MADE OF ALNWICK IN HIS EXPEDITION TO SCOTLAND WITH THE ARMY, 1639	109
PLATONICK LOVE	114
A MEDITATION UPON HIS WAX CANDLE BURNING OUT	119
OCTOBER 14, 1664	122
IN STATUAM LIGNEAM OVERBURII	124
DE C. DE S.	124
EPITAPHIUM IN ANAGRAMMA NOMINIS SUI REDDOR UT HERBÆ	125
EPITAPH. IN SE ROMÆ FACTUM 1615	125
IN TUMULUM DOMINI FRANCISCI VERE	126
IN DIEM NATALITIUM, VIZ 3 MAR.	127
FOR A DYAL	127
IN ANSWER TO THE VERSES OF GUIET FOR THE PUCELLE D'ORLEANS, QUASI EXTEMPORE	128

Contents. xiii

	PAGE
IN ANSWER TO TILENUS WHEN I HAD THAT FATAL DEFLUXION IN MY HAND	129
DE HUGONE GROTIO, ARCA INCLUSO ET A CARCERE LIBERATO	129
PRO LAUREATO POETA	130
AD SERENISS. REGEM GUSTAVUM, A.D. 1631	132
EURYALE MŒRENS	134
MENSA LUSORIA, OR, A SHOVEL-BOARD TABLE TO MR. MASTER	135
CHARISSIMO, DOCTISSIMO JUCUNDISSIMOQUE JUXTIM AMICO THOMÆ MASTER	136

INTRODUCTION.

LORD HERBERT of Cherbury is one of the most interesting, and in many respects one of the most essentially original characters, in our Literary History. At once a philosopher and a politician, a man of the world and a man of letters, it was his lot to flourish at a crisis of no ordinary importance in philosophy, in politics, in literature. His youth was passed in the world of Hooker, Sydney, and Spenser. Before he died Hobbes had written the *Elementa Philosophica de Cive*, Barclay had published his *Argenis*, and Butler was collecting materials for *Hudibras*. He was a child of eight when Elizabeth addressed the soldiers at Tilbury Fort, and he lived to see Charles the First betrayed by the Scots to the English Commissioners. He was the friend of Donne and Ben Jonson; he was the correspondent of Grotius and Gassendi. He thus stood midway between two great eras, moving in both. In temper he belonged to the era of the Renaissance, in intellect he belonged to the era of Des Cartes and Hobbes. His own services to literature were important. His *De Veritate*, if it did not do much for the advancement of metaphyfical philofophy, was the work of a fearlefs, vigorous, and independent thinker, a work which exercifed confiderable influence on the progrefs of Free Enquiry, and was the firft attempt made, in this country at leaft, to reduce Deifm to a fyftem. His *Life and Reign of Henry VIII.* is an admirable piece of hiftorical compofition. His *Expeditio Buckinghami Ducis in Ream Infulam* is the beft account we have of that unhappy adventure; and his *Autobiography* is, if ever autobiography was, a treafure for all time.

Thus interefting by his furroundings, thus important in himfelf, we are the more attracted towards him becaufe of the fulnefs with which we are acquainted with the incidents of his perfonal hiftory. We know him as we know no other man of that age. Never fince Jerome Cardan laid bare for the world's infpection the innermoft fecrets of his being, never fince Cellini told the ftory of his ftrange viciffitudes, never fince Montaigne took Europe into his confidence, had fuch a record as Herbert has left us been committed to paper. Whether he intended his fingular confeffions for publication may well be doubted. He tells us himfelf that they were written for the inftruction of his defcendents, and to enable him to review his paft career, that he might reform what was amifs if fuch reformation were poffible, that he might comfort himself with the memory of whatever virtuous actions he might have done, and that he might make his peace with God. In the course of this review he not only narrates the adventures which he had encountered on his way through life, but he enters into minute particulars relating to his writings and speculations—his struggles with his passions, his struggles with his reason he gives us his opinions on education, on the conduct of life, on religion And he is to all appearance unreserved His frailties are not concealed, and they are many; but we feel that he has, on the whole, gained rather than lost by a scrutiny which few, indeed, of our erring race could court with impunity. Nor is this all It is the portrait of a man with features eminently striking and peculiar, whose ways were never the ways of common men, whose thoughts were not the thoughts either of his predecessors or contemporaries. Nothing, therefore, which Herbert has left us can be without importance; for, whatever be its intrinsic value, it is the product of an original mind developing itself under exceptionally interesting historical conditions.

The world has long done justice to his prose writings. It is the object of the present volume to vindicate his title to a place among English poets. I have certainly no wish to be numbered among those gentlemen whose indiscriminating industry continues year after year to load our libraries with treasures better hidden. I have no wish to rob Oblivion of its legitimate prey. Some of Lord Herbert's poems are, I freely admit, not worth resuscitation, but many of them, or portions at least of many of them, seem to me authentic poetry. In almost all of them we find originality and vigour, however fantastic the conception, however rough the execution. But were their merits even less than they are, no cultivated man could regard them with indifference. The name of their writer would be a sufficient passport to indulgent attention. We treasure the verses of the authors of the *Nicomachæan Ethics,* and of the *Novum Organon,* though Aristotle has no claim to a place among the Pleiad, or Bacon to a place beside Jonson or Donne.

In my estimate of Lord Herbert's poems I have hitherto stood alone. His biographers and critics are unanimous in ignoring or condemning them. Antony Wood passes them by without comment. Horace Walpole merely mentions them in his Catalogue of Herbert's Works. Neither Grainger nor the author of the life in the *Biographie Universelle* have anything to say for them. Park, in a note on Walpole's *Life of Herbert,* coldly speaks of 'Lord Herbert's scarce volume of metaphysical love verses, ingenious but unnatural, platonic in sentiment, but frequently gross in expression, and marked by an eccentricity which pervaded the life and character of their author;' and these remarks have been greedily copied into successive editions of bibliographic manuals, reprints, and the like. Ellis, in his *Specimens of English Poetry*, is still less favourable in his verdict, boldly observing that young Herbert 'showed more piety than taste in publishing his father's poems.' The author of an article on the *Autobiography* in the *Retrospective Review* contents himself with remarking that Lord Herbert is often 'both rugged and obscure in his verses,' and 'was much more fitted to wield the sword than the lyre.' They have no place in the *Selections* of Headley. Even Campbell, who can find a niche for Heminge and Picke, has no corner for Herbert. M. Charles de Rémusat, in his interesting and valuable treatise, *Lord Herbert of Cherbury, sa Vie et ses Œuvres*, expresses similar opinions: 'Ses poésies anglaises, publiées par son second fils, sont d'un genre moins serieux '—(he has been speaking, and speaking depreciatingly, of Herbert's Latin poems)—' Quelques unes sont ingenieuses, la pluspart obscures; l'amour en est le sujet ordinaire, un amour platonique, exprimé cependant avec plus de recherche que délicatesse.' It is curious that they should have escaped the notice of Sir Egerton Brydges, who has not, so far as I can discover, made any allusion to them. And this is the more remarkable, as he was particularly interested in the history of the Herbert family, and was the first editor of the poems of William Herbert, third Earl of Pembroke. When he obferved in the preface to his reprint of the Earl's poems that 'to fuffer them to lie longer in oblivion would be to defraud an illuftrious family of its greateft ornaments,' he made a remark which would be far more applicable to the prefent volume. Whatever opinion may be formed of Lord Herbert's merits as a poet, there can be no queftion as to his fuperiority to his kinfman

It is ftrange that in his *Autobiography* Lord Herbert makes no mention of his Poems, the exiftence of which feems not to have been fufpected by any of his diftinguifhed contemporaries. They were evidently jotted down in moments of leifure, as occafion offered. Some of them were the work of his youth, fome of his middle age; the laft was written four years before his death. This we gather from the dates prefixed to many of them, the earlieft date being Auguft 1608, the lateft October 1664. The biographers affure us that many of thefe poems had appeared in print during Herbert's lifetime, and are to be found in the poetical collections of the period. For thefe collections I have fearched in vain. I doubt, I muft own, the truth of the ftatement, and fufpect that it has been loofely copied, without any attempt to afcertain its correctnefs, from Antony Wood; and I am the more inclined to believe this becaufe they have faithfully repeated one grofs blunder of Wood's—a blunder which would at once have been rectified by confulting the work to which Wood refers. It is this, and it is fignificant. In the third volume of his *Athenæ Oxonienfes* (edition Blifs, p. 242) Wood fays: 'Other of Lord Herbert's poems I have feen in the books of other authors occafionally written, particularly in that of Jofhua Sylvefter, entitled *Lacrymæ Lacrymarum*, 1613.' This affertion is repeated by Walpole, by Sir Walter Scott in the Prefatory Memoir to Lord Herbert's *Autobiography*, publifhed at Edinburgh in 1809, by the editor of Murray's reprint of the *Life*, and by all the bibliographers. Now there is not a line of Lord Herbert's to be found in Sylvefter's work. What Wood was thinking of was no doubt the *Elegy for the Prince* (fee Poems, page 33), which certainly was publifhed during Herbert's lifetime, but which appeared, not in Sylvefter's *Lacrymæ Lacrymarum*, but in a collection entitled *Sundry Funeral Elegies on the Untimely Death of the Moft Excellent Prince Henry*, compofed by feveral hands, 1613. However this may be, the poems made their appearance in a collected form in 1665, nearly feventeen years after Herbert's death; and were, as we learn from the Preface, given to the world by Henry Herbert, his youngeft fon. Of thefe poems there appears to have been only one edition. The volume is now extremely rare; indeed, it is one of the rareft known to bibliographers.

The reader will at once discover that Herbert belongs, like his brother, to that school of poets whose characteristics have been so admirably analysed by Johnson—the Metaphysical or Phantastic School. This singular sect first appeared during the latter years of Elizabeth's reign. Their origin is popularly ascribed to Dr. Donne, though it would in truth be more correct to say that in the poetry of Donne their peculiarities of sentiment and expression are most conspicuously illustrated. They owed their origin, indeed, not to the influence of Donne, but to the spirit of the age. In all eras of great creative energy poetry passes necessarily through two stages: in the first stage, imagination predominates; in the second, reflection. In the first stage, men feel more than they think; in the second, they think more than they feel. If a literature run its natural course, we may predict with absolute certainty that mere rhetoric will usurp the place of the eloquent language of the passions, that fancy will be substituted for imagination, and that there will cease to be any necessary correspondence between the emotions and the intellect. This stage was not completely attained till the age of Cowley. In the poetry of Donne we find the transition between the two stages marked with singular precision. Some of his poems remind us of the richest and freshest work of the Elizabethan age; in many of them he out-Cowleys Cowley himself. But his work was not the work, in any fenfe, of a creator. He contributed no new elements, either to thought or to diction. What he did was to unite the vicious peculiarities of others, to indulge habitually in what they indulged in only occafionally. He was not, for example, the firft to fubftitute philofophical reflection for poetic feeling, as his contemporaries, Samuel Daniel, Sir John Davies, and Fulke Greville, were fimultaneoufly engaged in doing the fame thing. He was not the firft to indulge in abufe of wit, in fanciful fpeculations, in extravagant imagery, or in grotefque eccentricities of expreffion. But, in addition to uniting thefe vices, he carried them further than any of his predeceffors or contemporaries had done, and, aided by the fpirit of the age, he fucceeded in making them popular. It would not, perhaps, be faying too much to fay that no fingle author contributed more to the foundation of the Metaphyfical School than Jofhua Sylvefter, whofe tranflation of Du Bartas preceded the 'metaphyfical' poems of Donne, and was probably as favourite a work with Donne as it certainly was with moft of the young poets of that age. The ftyle of Donne is, however, marked by certain diftinctive peculiarities which no intelligent critic would be likely to miftake, and his influence on contemporary poetry was unqueftionably confiderable. Lord Herbert appears to have been the earlieft of his difciples. Indeed, moft of the poems in Herbert's collection in which the influence of Donne is most perceptible, had been written, as the dates show, long before the poems of Donne were given to the world. But he was, we know, personally acquainted with Donne, and Donne, like many of the poets of that age, was in the habit of circulating copies of his poems among private friends.* His acquaintance with his master commenced, no doubt, while he was still a student at University College; for we learn from Walton's *Life of George Herbert* that when Mrs. Herbert was living with her son Edward at Oxford Donne arrived there on a visit, and became, during her residence at Oxford, one of her most valued friends and advisers His beautiful poem entitled the *Autumnal* was written in honour of Mrs. Herbert As Herbert was then a youth of eighteen, and Donne a man of upwards of forty, it is not unreasonable to suppose that Donne assisted both in moulding the youth's tastes and in directing his studies.

Where Herbert most reminds us of Donne is not

---

* Dr Grosart, in his laborious and instructive account of Donne and his writings, tells us that several of Donne's descriptive and satirical poems were in circulation among friends certainly before 1614, and that some of his lyrics were in circulation before 1613. (See his remarks on his edition of Donne, vol ii, *Essay on the Life and Writings of Donne*, pp. xxxi. and xxxii)

so much in his lyrics as in his poems written in the heroic measures; in the two satires, for example, in the verses 'To his Mistress for her True Picture,' in the elegy on Donne himself. The poem also entitled 'The Idea' is very much in his friend's vein, as well as written in a measure which Donne perhaps invented, and which was certainly a favourite with him. The numerous poems dedicated to the praise of dark beauty were perhaps suggested by Donne's verses *To a Lady of Dark Complexion*. In the two poems on Platonic Love we may also discern the presence of the master. It would, of course, be absurd to assert that the lyric poetry of Donne had no influence on that of Herbert, but its influence was far less considerable than it would at first sight appear to be. Herbert's rhythm is his own. Where it is musical its music is not the music of the older poet, where its note is harsh and dissonant it is no echo of the discords of that unequal and most capricious singer. Many of Donne's favourite measures he has not employed, some of his own measures, the measures in which he has been most successful, have no prototype in Donne's poems. What he owes in lyric poetry to the leader of the Metaphysical School is to be found, so far as form is concerned, rather in what Donne suggested than in what he directly taught In spirit he owed, it must be allowed, much From Donne he learned to sport with extravagant fancies, to

c

substitute the language of the schools for the language of the heart, to think like the author of the *Enneads* and to write like the author of *Euphues*. He has, however, had the good taste to avoid the grosser faults of his master. He never indulges in preposterous absurdities, he never, if we except one couplet, clothes mysticism in motley.

Herbert's poems are of too miscellaneous a character to be exactly classified. They may be roughly divided into Sonnets, Elegies, Epitaphs, Satires, Miscellaneous Lyrics, and Occasional Pieces. However unequal these compositions may be in point of execution, there are two things which the reader of Herbert may, in the more ambitious poems at least, generally promise himself—originality and vigour. The Sonnets need not detain us long. The one 'To his Watch' (page 1) is well expressed. The style is in happy unison with the sentiment, and the final clause is solemn and impressive. The last verse of the sonnet 'To her Face' (page 6),

'Sure Adam sinn'd not in that spotless face,'

though somewhat obscure, is a really fine line. In the sonnet written near Merlou Castle (page 12), the couplet describing the groves on the banks of the stream,

'Embroidering through each glade
An airy silver and a sunny gold,'

prove that Herbert had the eye of a poet. The moſt ſtriking of them is the addreſs 'To Black Itſelf' (page 59), which is particularly intereſting, becauſe it contains the germ of part at leaſt of the idea which was afterwards ſo magnificently embodied by Blanco White in his famous ſonnet. White was moſt likely immediately indebted to Sir Thomas Browne, but Browne was no doubt well acquainted with Herbert and his writings. With regard to his Elegies—I am not, of courſe, including among them the lyric elegy on page 49—I ſhall perhaps conſult his fame beſt by paſſing them by without comment. Two or three verſes in the 'Elegy on the Prince' will no doubt pleaſe and ſtrike, but there praiſe muſt end, even from an editor. Of the Epitaphs, the moſt original is the 'Epitaph upon Himſelf' (page 81), the moſt groteſque that on Cecilia Boulfer (page 29), the moſt eloquent and pleaſing that on William Herbert of Swanſey (page 31). The two ſatires are of very unequal merit. The ſecond, page 20, would diſgrace Taylor the Water Poet. The firſt, 'The State Progreſs of Ill,' though intolerably harſh and barbarous in ſtyle, contains ſome intereſting remarks. Of the Occaſional Pieces, thoſe which moſt nearly reſembled the poems of which we have been ſpeaking are the verſes entitled 'To her Mind' (page 8), and 'To his Miſtreſs for her True Picture' (page 74), both being in the heroic couplet, and both being in the ſame contemplative vein. To those who are fond of tracing resemblances between the works of men of genius who are separated by many years from each other, it will be interesting to observe how closely Herbert sometimes reminds us of Mr. Browning. In the verses, for example, 'To her Mind,' there is a passage which might excusably be mistaken for the work of the great philosophical poet of our day —

> 'Thus ends my Love, but this doth grieve me most
> That so it ends; but that ends too, this yet,
> Beside the wishes, hopes and time I lost,
> Troubles my mind awhile, that I am set
> Free, worse than deny'd. I can neither boast
> Choice nor success, as my case is, nor get
> Pardon from myself, that I loved not
> A better mistress, or her worse. This debt
> Only's her due, still that she be forgot
> Ere chang'd, lest I love none; this done, the taint
> Of foul inconstancy is cleared at least
> In me, there only rests but to unpaint
> Her form in my mind, that so dispossess'd,
> It be a temple, but without a saint'

— the same elliptical mode of expression, the same intermixture of sentiment and logic, the same curious refinements of speculative meditation. The verses 'To his Mistress for her True Picture' will not find, and they certainly do not deserve, many admirers. It may be questioned whether Platonism has ever clothed itself in such grotesque language as in the last couplet of this strange poem:

> ' Hear from my body's prison this my call,
> Who from my mouth-grate and eye-window bawl '

The lyric pieces are of very unequal merit. But in making out a case for Herbert my business is only with his best work, and if we judge him by his best work, he is certainly entitled to no mean place among the lyrists of the Metaphysical School. His music is, it must be owned, full of discords—his verses will sometimes not even scan, and yet he possessed not only a fine ear for rhythmic effect, but his rhythm is of great compass and variety. Occasionally his verse has a weight, a fullness and dignity, not unworthy of Dryden; for example, two stanzas like these (pages 10 and 11):

> ' Nay, thou art greater, too!   More destiny
>   Depends on thee than on her influence.
>   No hair thy fatal hand doth now dispense
> But to some one a thread of life must be.

   *   *   *   *   *

> ' But stay! methinks new beauties do arise
>   While she withdraws these glories which were spread.
>   Wonder of Beauties! set thy radiant head,
> And strike out Day from thy yet fairer eyes '

Nor can we refuse the gift of lyric melody to the writer of a stanza like this —

> 'Then think each minute that you lose a day,
>   The longest youth is short,
> The shortest age is long : Time flies away,
>   And makes us but his sport,
> And that which is not Youth's is Age's prey.'

Or to the writer of such poems as we find on page 56, and on page 46.

But Herbert's greatest metrical triumph is that he was the first to discover the harmony of that stanza with which the most celebrated poet of our own day has familiarised us. The glory of having invented it belongs indeed to another, but the glory of having passed it almost perfect into Mr. Tennyson's hands belongs unquestionably to Herbert And it is due also to Herbert to say that he not only revealed its sweetness and beauty, but that he anticipated some of its most exquisite effects and variations. Take, for example, the following stanza, where the pause occurs at the end of the second line.—

> ' For where affection once is shown,
>   No longer can the World beguile ;
>   Who sees his penance all the while
> He holds a torch to make her known '—*Ditty*, page 42

Or these lines, where the pause is made at the end of the first line :—

> 'Else should our souls in vain elect,
>   And vainer yet were Heaven's laws
>   When to an everlasting cause
> They give a perishing effect.'—Page 96.

Or again —

> 'Nay, I protest ; though Death with his
>   Worst counsel should divide us here ,'—Page 94.

where the pause occurs at the end of the fourth syllable. An analytical examination of the metre of *In Memoriam* will show that on alternations and interchanges of those pauses the poet has not only relied for varying his harmony, but for producing some of his most pleasing effects. Indeed, in Herbert's two poems we find anticipated the exact cadence, the exact note of the modern poet I question, for example, whether the nicest ear could distinguish lines like these from the Laureate's .—

> 'Were not our souls immortal made,
>   Our equal loves can make them such.'

> 'As one another's mystery,
> Each shall be both, yet both but one.'

> 'Who sees his penance all the while
> He holds a torch to make her known.'

Other points of resemblance, into which there is no

necessity for entering here, can scarcely fail to suggest themselves to thoughtful readers. It is curious that we should be able to point—and to point, I venture to think, without at all straining analogy—to two poems of this forgotten poet which recall so exactly the work of the author of *In Memoriam* and the work of the author of *Sordello*. If the circumstance prove little else, it proves at least the versatility of Herbert's powers.

The best of Herbert's lyrics is the poem of which we have just been speaking—the 'Ode upon a Question moved whether Love should Continue for Ever.' It is a little prolix, and it is occasionally obscure, but the finest stanzas in it are exquisitely beautiful. Next would come, in the estimation of many perhaps, the verses 'Upon combing her Hair' (page 10), which are singularly vigorous and picturesque. We feel, however, that their sounding rhetoric is somewhat out of place—the style is too elevated for the theme, a common fault with poets of the second order. Among other lyrics of a serious cast the 'Elegy over a Tomb' (page 49) and the verses 'To her Hair' (page 56) deserve mention. Of the lighter lyrics the 'Ditty in Imitation of the Spanish' will probably be read with much pleasure. The Platonic Love poems, though not without interest and even merit, cannot be said to hold a very high rank among poems of the class to which they belong. With one exception—the ode on page 92, to which I have already referred—they are little calculated either to pleafe or to ftrike. They have all the frigidity and pedantic ingenuity of Petrarch and Bembo without thofe beauties of expreffion which ftill attract us in the Sonnetti and Canzoni 'The Idea' is, however, well worth attentive perufal. Rarely have the doctrines of pure Platonifm been more fkilfully applied, rarely have philofophy and fentiment been more ingenioufly blended.

Herbert's moft confpicuous defects, both in thefe and in his other poems, are want of finifh and exceffive obfcurity. He feldom does juftice to his conceptions. He had evidently no love for the labour of the file, and he has paid, like Donne and Fulke Greville, the juft penalty for his careleffnefs

The Latin poems of Herbert are fcarcely likely to find favour in the eyes of modern fcholars Their diction is, as a rule, involved and obfcure, they teem with forced and unclaffical expreffions. His hendecafyllabics are intolerably harfh, and violate almoft every metrical canon. His Elegiacs are not more fuccefsful, indeed, the only tolerable copy among the poemata are the verfes on a Dial, for the epigrams are below contempt. In his hexameters he fucceeds better. The 'Menfa Luforia' is ingenious and not inelegant, and the 'Pro Laureato Poetâ,' though unneceffarily obfcure, is, like the epiftle to Guftavus, extremely fpirited But even at his beft he cannot for an inftant be compared with his contemporaries, Owen, Milton, Cowley, or May, who wrote Latin, nor indeed with the purity of the poets of the Italian Renaiffance, but with wonderful fluency and vigour. Befide the Latin poems appearing in this volume, Herbert was the author of three others, entitled refpectively 'Hæredibus ac Nepotibus fuis Præcepta,' which is in elegiacs, 'De Vitâ Humanâ Philofophica Difquifitio,' and 'De Vitâ Cœlefti ex ejufdem principiis Conjectura,' which are in hexameters. They are to be found among certain tracts appended to the *De Caufis Errorum*, printed in 1645.* The two laft appear alfo in the *Autobiography*, and they are by far the beft. But as thefe poems are not likely to intereft readers in our day, and poffefs little or no value in themfelves, we have refrained from adding them, even by way of appendix, to the prefent volume.

---

* The exact title of the volume is, *De Caufis Errorum, una cum tractatu De Religione Laici et Appendice ad Sacerdotes, necnon quibufdam poematibus.* *Londini*, 1645 (Walpole fays, erroneoufly, 1647)

OCCASIONAL VERSES

OF

EDWARD LORD HERBERT

BARON

OF

CHERBURY AND CASTLE-ISLAND.

Deceased in August 1648.

LONDON.
Printed by T. R. *for* THOMAS DRING,
At THE GEORGE *in* FLEET STREET, *near* CLIFFORD'S INN
1665

To the
Right Hon. Edward Lord Herbert,
Baron of Cherbery in England and Castle Island in Ireland.

My Lord,

This Collection of some of the scattered Copies of Verses, composed in various and perplexed times, by Edward Lord Herbert, your late Grandfather, belongs of double right to your Lordship, as Heir and Executor, and had it been in his power to have bequeathed his Learning by Will, as his Library and Personal Estate, it may be presumed he would have given it to you as the best Legacy. But Learning being not of our Gift, though of our Acquisition, nor of the Parapharnalia of a Lady's Chamber, nor of the casual and fortunate Goods of the World, it must be acknowledged of a transcendency beyond natural things, and a beam of the Divinity. For by the Powers of Knowledge Men are not only distinguished from Men, but carried above the reach of ordinary Persons, to give Reasons even of their Belief—not that men believe because they know, but know because they believe. Faith must precede Knowledge; and yet men are not bound to accept matters of Religion, though Religion be the object and employment of faith, not of reasoning merely without Reason and probable Inducements.

That the learned Centuries are past, and Learning in declension, is too great a truth, which may introduce Atheisme with Ignorance; for as Ignorance is the Mother of Devotion amongst the Papists, so 'tis the Mother of Atheisme amongst the Ignorant.

The great and most dangerous design of our Church and National Enemies, is to make us out of Love with Learning, as a Mechanick thing and beneath the Spirits of the Nobility and of Princes: whereas nothing improves and enlightens the understandings of great Persons but Learning, and not only ennobles them far above their birth, but enables them to impose on others, and to give rather than take advice. The Learned, Generous, and Vertuous Person needs no

Ancestors. And what can so properly be call'd ours as what is of our purchase?

'Gentiles agunt sub nomine Christiano' *was an old Reproach upon the Primitive Christians; and now Men out-act the Gentiles.*

The Goods of this life are all Hydropick, Quo plus bibuntur, plus sitiuntur. *Men are the drier for drinking and the poorer for covetousness: no satiety, no fulness, but in spiritual things. The way of Vertue appeared to the Heathen to be the only way to Happiness, and yet they knew not many vertues which are the Glory of Christianity, as Humility, Denying of our selves, Taking up the Cross, forgiving and loving our Enemies, which the Heathen took for follies rather than Vertues.*

As for Poetry, it bears date before Prose, and was of so great authority with the common People and the wiser sort of antiquity, that it was in veneration with their Sacred Writ and Records, from which they derived their divinity and belief concerning their Gods, and that their Poets, as Orpheus, Linus, and Musæus, were descended of the Gods, and divinely inspired, from the extra-

ordinary Motions of their Minds, and from the Relations of strange Visions, Raptures, and Apparitions.

My Lord, excuse the liberty of this Dedication, and believe me,

   Your Lordship's Uncle
    and Humble Servant,
      HENRY HERBERT.

March 18th, 166$\frac{4}{5}$.

OCCASIONAL VERSES.

TO HIS WATCH
WHEN HE COULD NOT SLEEP.

UNCESSANT Minutes, whilst you move you tell
   The time that tells our life, which, though it run
  Never so fast or far, your new begun
Short steps shall overtake; for though life well

May scape his own Account, it shall not yours
   You are Death's Auditors, that both divide
And sum what ere that life inspir'd endures
   Past a beginning, and through you we bide

The doom of Fate, whose unrecall'd Decree
   You date, bring, execute; making what's new
  Ill, and good old, for as we die in you,
You die in Time, Time in Eternity

DITTY.

DEEP Sighs, Records of my unpitied Grief,
    Memorials of my true though hopeless Love,
Keep time with my sad thoughts, till wish'd Relief
My long despairs for vain and causless prove.
Yet if such hap never to you befall,
I give you leave, break time, break heart, and all.

Lord, thus I sin, repent, and sin again,
As if Repentance only were in me
Leave for new Sin, thus do I entertain
My short time, and Thy Grace, abusing Thee
And Thy long suffering, which, though it be
Ne'er overcome by Sin, yet were in vain
If tempted oft: thus we our Errors see

Before our Punishment, and so remain
Without Excuse: and, Lord, in them 'tis true
Thy Laws are just, but why dost Thou distrain
Ought else for life save life? That is Thy due,
The rest Thou mak'st us owe, and may'st to us
As well forgive. But, oh! my sins renew,
Whilst I do talk with my Creator thus.

A DESCRIPTION.

*I SING her worth and praises, I,
   Of whom a Poet cannot lie.
The little World the Great shall blaze,
Sea, Earth, her Body, Heaven, her Face,
Her Hair, Sunbeams, whose every part
Lightens, inflames each Lover's Heart,
That thus you prove the †Axiom true,
Whilst the Sun helped Nature in you
Her Front, the white and azure sky
In Light and Glory raised high,
Being o'recast by a cloudy frown,
All Hearts and Eyes dejecteth down,
Her each Brow, a celestial Bow
Which through this Sky her Light doth show,
Which doubled, if it strange appear
The Sun's likewise is doubled there,
Her either Cheek, a blushing Morn,
Which, on the Wings of Beauty born,
Doth never set, but only fair
Shineth exalted in her hair;*

---

* μικρόκοσμος μακροκόσμος. † *Sol et homo generant hominem.*

A Description.

Within her Mouth Heaven's Heav'n reside,
Her words the souls there Glorifi'd;
Her Nose, th' Æquator of this Globe,
Where Nakedness, Beauty's best Robe,
Presents a form all Hearts to win.
Last Nature made that Dainty Chin,
Which that it might in every fashion
Answer the rest, a Constellation
Like to a Desk, She there did place
To write the Wonders of her Face.
In this Cœlestial Frontispiece,
Where Happiness eternal lies,
First arranged stand three Senses,—
This Heaven's Intelligences,
Whose several Motions sweet combined
Come from the first Mover, her Mind.
The weight of this Harmonique Sphere
The Atlas of her Neck doth bear,
Whose favours Day to Us imparts
When Frowns make Night in Lovers' Hearts.
Two foaming Billows are her Breasts,
That carry rais'd upon their Crests
The Tyrian Fish. More white's their Foam
Then that whence Venus once did come.
Here take her by the Hand, my Muse,
With that Sweet Foe, to make my Truce,

A Description.

To compact Manna best compar'd,
Whose dewy inside's not full hard.
Her Waist's an envers'd Pyramis
Upon whose Cone Love's Trophy is.
Her Belly is that Magazine
At whose peep Nature did resigne
That precious Mould by which alone
There can be framed such a One:
At th' entrance of which hidden Treasure,
Happy making above measure,
Two Alabaster Pillars stand,
To warn all passage from that Land,
At foot whereof engraved is
The sad *Non Ultra* of Man's Bliss.
The back of this most pretious Frame
Holds up in Majesty the Same;
Where to make Music to all Hearts
Love bound the descant of her parts.
Though all this Beauty's Temple be
There's known within no Deity
Save Virtues shrin'd within her Will.
As I began, so say I still,
I sing her Worth and Praises, I,
Of whom a Poet cannot lie

TO HER FACE.

FATAL Aspect! that hast an influence
  More powerful far than those Immortal Fires
That but incline the Will and move the Sense
Which thou alone constrainst, kindling desires
Of such a holy force, as more inspires
The Soul with Knowledge, than Experience
Or Revelation can do with all
Their borrow'd helps: Sacred Astonishment
Sits on thy Brow, threat'ning a sudden fall
To all those Thoughts that are not lowly sent
In wonder and amaze, dazzling that Eye
Which on those Mysteries doth rudely gaze
Vow'd only unto Love's Divinity:
Sure Adam sinn'd not in that spotless Face.

TO HER BODY

REGARDFUL Presence! whose fix'd Majesty
    Darts Admiration on the gazing Look
That brings it not: State sits enthron'd in thee,
Divulging forth her Laws in the fair Book
Of thy Commandements, which none mistook
That ever humbly came therein to see
Their own unworthiness. Oh, how can I
Enough admire that Symmetry, exprest
In new Proportions, which doth give the Lie
To that Arithmetic which hath profest
All Numbers to be Hers? Thy Harmony
Comes from the Spheres, and there doth prove
Strange measures, so well grac'd, as Majesty
Itself like thee would rest, like thee would move.

TO HER MIND.

EXALTED Mind! Whose character doth bear
  The first idea of Perfection, whence
Adam's came, and stands so. How can'st appear
In words that only tell what here-
Tofore hath been? Thou need'st as deep a sense
As Prophecy, since there's no difference
In telling what thou art and what shalt be.
Then pardon me that Rapture do profess
At thy outside, that want for what I see
Description of. Here amaz'd I cease
Thus——
Yet grant one question and no more, crav'd under
Thy gracious leave: How, if thou wouldst express
Thyself to us, thou shouldst be still a wonder?

Thus ends my Love, but this doth grieve me most
That so it ends; but that ends too; this yet,
Besides the Wishes, hopes, and time I lost,
Troubles my mind awhile, that I am set

To her Mind.

Free, worse than denied: I can neither boast
Choice nor Success as my Case is, nor get
Pardon from myself, that I loved not
A better Mistress, or her worse.   This Debt
Only's her due, still that she be forgot
Ere chang'd, lest I love none: this done, the taint
Of foul Inconstancy is clear'd at least.
In me, there only rests but to unpaint
Her form in my mind, that so dispossest,
It be a Temple, but without a Saint.

UPON COMBING HER HAIR.

BREAKING from under that thy cloudy Veil
   Open and ſhine yet more, ſhine out more clear,
Thou glorious golden-beam-darting hair,
Even till my wonder-ſtricken Senſes fail.

Shoot out in light, and ſhine thoſe Rays on far,
Thou much more fair than is the Queen of Love,
When ſhe doth comb her in her Sphere above,
And from a Planet turns a Blazing Star.

Nay, thou art greater, too! More deſtiny
Depends on thee than on her influence.
No hair thy fatal hand doth now diſpenſe,
But to ſome one a thred of life muſt be.

While gracious unto me thou both doſt ſunder
Thoſe glories which, if they united were,
Might have amazed ſenſe, and ſhew'ſt each hair
Which, if alone, had been too great a wonder

Upon Combing her Hair.

And now spread in their goodly length, sh' appears
No creature which the earth might call her own,
But rather one that, in her gliding down,
Heav'ns beams did crown, to shew us she was theirs.

And come from thence, how can they fear Time's rage,
Which in his power else on earth most strange,
Such golden treasure doth to Silver change
By that improper Alchemy of Age?

But stay! methinks new Beauties do arise
While she withdraws these Glories which were spread·
Wonder of Beauties! set thy radiant head,
And strike out Day from thy yet fairer eyes.

DITTY IN IMITATION OF THE SPANISH ENTRE TANTOQUE EL'AVRIL.

NOW that the April of your youth adorns
   The garden of your face,
Now that for you each knowing Lover mourns,
   And all seek to your grace,
Do not repay affection with scorns.

What though you may a matchless Beauty vaunt,
   And all that Hearts can move
By such a power that seemeth to enchant,
   Yet, without help of Love,
Beauty no pleasure to itself can grant.

Then think each minute that you lose a day.
   The longest youth is short,
The shortest Age is long, Time flies away,
   And makes us but his sport,
And that which is not Youth's is Age's prey.

Ditty.

See but the braveſt Horſe that prideth moſt,
    Though he eſcaped the War,
Either from Maſter to the Man, is loſt,
    Or turned unto the Car;
Or elſe muſt die with being ridden Poſt.

Then loſe not Beauty, Lovers, Time, and all,
    Too late your fault you ſee,
When that in vain you would theſe days recall.
    Nor can you virtuous be,
When without theſe you have not wherewithal.

THE STATE-PROGRESS OF ILL.

I SAY, 'tis hard to write Satires. Though Ill
   Great'ned in his long courſe, and ſwelling ſtill,
Be now like to a Deluge, yet, as Nile,
'Tis doubtful in his original. This while
We may thus much on either part preſume,
That what ſo univerſal are, muſt come
From cauſes great and far. Now in this State
Of things, which is leaſt like good, Men hate,
Since 'twill be the leſs ſin. I do ſee
Some ill required, that one poiſon might free
The other, ſo ſtates, to their Greatneſs, find
No faults required but their own, and bind
The reſt. And though this be myſterious, ſtill,
Why ſhould we not imagine how this Ill
Did come at firſt, how't keeps his greatneſs here,
When 'tis diſguiſ'd, and when it doth appear.
This Ill, having ſome attributes of God
As to have made it ſelf and bear the rod
Of all our puniſhments, as it ſeems, came

The State-Progress of Ill.

Into the World to rule it, and to tame
The pride of Goodness, and though his Reign
Great in the hearts of men he doth maintain
By love, not right, he yet the tyrant here
(Though it be him we love and God we fear),
Pretence yet wants not, that it was before
Some part of Godhead, as Mercy, that store
For Souls grown Bankrupt, their first stock of Grace,
And that which the sinner of the last place
Shall number out, unless th' Highest will show
Some power not yet reveal'd to Man below.

But that I may proceed, and so go on
To trace Ill in his first progression,
And through his Secret'st ways, and where that he
Had left his nakedness as well as we,
And did appear himself,
   I note that in $\left.\begin{array}{l}\\\\\end{array}\right\}$ Gradus mali sunt quo $\left\{\begin{array}{l}\text{Peccamus nobis.}\\\text{Nocemus aliis.}\end{array}\right.$
The yet infant world how
   Mischief and sin,
His Agents here on earth, and easy known,
Are now concealed Intelligencers grown
For since that as a Guard th' Highest at once
Put Fear t' attend their private actions,
And Shame their publick, other means being fail'd,
Mischief under doing of Good was veil'd,

The State-Progress of Ill.

And Sin, of Pleasure, though in this disguise
They only hide themselves from mortal eyes
Sins, those that both com- and o-mitted be,
Once hot and cold, but in a third degree
Are now such poisons, that though they may lurk
In secret parts awhile, yet they will work
Though after death; nor ever come alone,
But sudden-fruitful multiply ere done.
While in this monstrous birth they only die
Whom we confess, those live which we deny.
Mischiefs, like fatal Constellations,
Appear unto the ignorant at once
In glory and in hurt, while th'unseen part
Of the great cause may be perchance the Art
Of th' Ill and hiding it, which that I may
Ev'n in his first original display,
And best example, sure amongst Kings, he,
Who first wanted successions to be,
A Tyrant was, wise enough to have chose
An honest man for King, which should dispose
Those beasts, which being so tame, yet otherwise
As it seems, could not herd, And with advise
Somewhat indifferent for both, he might
Yet have provided for their Children's right,
If they grew wiser, not his own, that so
They might repent, yet under treason, who

The State-Progress of Ill.

Ne'er promis'd faith: though now we cannot spare
(And not be worse) Kings, on those terms, they are
No worse than we could spare (and have been sav'd)
Original sin. So then those Priests that rav'd
And prophesy'd, they did a kind of good
They knew not of, by whom the choice first stood.
    Since, then, we may consider now as fit
State government, and all the Acts of it,
That we may know them yet, let us see how
They were derived, done, and are maintained now,
That Princes may by this yet understand
Why we obey as well as they command.
State a proportion'd colour'd table is,
Nobility the master-piece in this,
Serves to shew distances; while being put
'Twixt sight and vastness they seem higher, but
As they're further off; yet as those blue hills
Which th' utmost border of a Region fills,
They are great and worse parts, while in the steep
Of this great Prospective they seem to keep
Further absent from those below, though this
Exalted Spirit, that's sure a free Soul, is
A greater Privilege than to be born
At Venice, although he seek not rule, doth scorn
Subjection, but as he is flesh, and so
He is to dulness, shame, and many moe

The State-Progress of Ill.

Such properties, knows, but the Painter's Art,
All in the frame is equal.   That desert
Is a more living thing, and doth obey
As he gives poor, for God's sake (though they
And Kings ask it not so), thinks Honours are
Figures compos'd of lines irregular,
And happy-high knows no election
Raiseth man to true Greatness but his own
Meanwhile sugar'd Divines, next place to this,
Tell us Humility and Patience is
The way to Heaven, and that we must there
Look for our Kingdom, that the great'st rule here
Is for to rule ourselves   And that they might
Say this the better, they to no place have right
B'inheritance, while whom Ambition sways,
Their office is to turn it other ways.
  Those yet, whose harder minds Religion
Cannot invade, nor turn from thinking on
A present greatness, that combin'd curse of Law
Of officers' and Neighbours' spite doth draw
Within such whirlpools, that till they be drown'd
They ne'er get out, but only swim them round
    Thus brief, since that the infinite of ill
Is neither easie told nor safe, I will
But only note how freeborn Man, subdu'd
By his own choice, that was at first endu'd

The State-Progress of Ill.

With equal power over all, doth now submit
That infinite of Number, Spirit, Wit,
To some eight Monarchs   Then why wonder Men
    Their rule of horses?
The world, as in the Ark of Noah, rests
Compos'd as then, few Men and many Beasts.

Aug 1608.
At Merlou in France

SATYRA SECUNDA

OF TRAVELLERS FROM PARIS

BEN JOHNSON, travel is a second birth
    Unto the Children of another Earth;
Only as our King Richard was, so they appear,
New born to another World, with teeth and hair
While got by English Parents, carried in
Some Womb of thirty-tun and lightly twin,
They are delivered at Calais or at Dieppe,
And strangely stand, go feed themselves, nay, keep
Their own money streightways, but that is all,
For none can understand them when they call
For anything. No more than Badger,
That call'd the Queen Monsieur, laid a wager
With the King of his Dogs who understood
Them all alike, which Badger thought was good.
But that I may proceed. Since their birth is
Only a kind of Metempsychosis,
Such Knowledge as their Memory could give
They have for help, what time these Souls do live
In English clothes, a body which again

Satyra Secunda.

They never rife unto, but, as you fee
When they come home, like children yet that be
Of their own bringing up; all they learn is
Toys and the Language, but to attain this
You muft conceive they're cofen'd, mocked, and come
To Fourbourgs St. Germans, there take a Room
Lightly about th' Ambaffadors, and where,
Having no Church, they come Sundays to hear
An invitation which they have moft part,
If their outfide but promife a defert,
To fit above the Secretaries' place,
Although it be almoft as rare a cafe
To fee Englifh well cloth'd here, as with you
At London, Indians. But that your view
May comprehend at once them gone for Blois
Or Orleans, learn'd French, now no more Boys
But perfect men at Paris, putting on
Some forc'd difguife, or labour'd fafhion,
To appear ftrange at home, befides their ftay,
Laugh and look on with me, to fee what they
Are now become, but that the poorer fort,
A fubject not fit for my Mufe nor fport,
May pafs untouch'd, let's but confider what
Elpus is now become, once young, handfome, and that
Was fuch a Wit, as very well with four
Of the fix might have made one, and no more,

Satyra Secunda.

Had he been at their Valentine, and could
Agree, your Rus ſhould uſe the ſtock who would
Carefully in that, ev'n as 'twere his own
Put out their Jeſts, briefly one that was grown
Ripe to another taſte than that wherein
He is now ſeaſoned and dry'd, as in
His face by this you ſee, which would perplex
A ſtranger to define his years, or ſex;
To which his wrinkles, when he ſpeaks doth give
That Age his words ſhould have, while he doth ſtrive,
As if ſuch births had never come from brain
To ſhew his mots deliver'd without pain,
Nor without After-throes.   Sometimes as grace
Did overflow in circles o're his face,
Ev'n to the brim, which he thinks ſure
If this poſture do but ſo long endure
That it be fix'd by Age he'll look as like
A ſpeaking ſign, as our St. George to ſtrike,
That, where he is, none but will hold their peace
If th' have but the leaſt good manners, or confeſs,
If he ſhould ſpeak, he did preſume too far
In ſpeaking then, when others readier are
Now that he ſpeaks are complemental ſpeeches
That never go off but below the breeches
Of him he doth ſalute, while he doth wring
And with ſome looſe French words which he doth ſtring,

Satyra Secunda.

Windeth about the arms, the legs and sides,
Most serpent-like of any man that bides
His indirect approach, which being done
Almost without an introduction,
If he have heard but any bragging French
Boast of the favor of some noble wench,
He'll swear 'twas he did her graces possess,
And damn his own soul for the wickedness
Of other men, strangest of all in that.
But I am weary to describe you what,
Ere this, you can. As for the little fry
That all along the street turn up the eye
At everything they meet, that have not yet
Seen that swol'n vicious Queen Margaret,
Who were a monster ev'n without her sin,
Nor the Italian comedies wherein
Women play Boys ——I cease to write.
To end this Satire and bid thee good Night.

Sept. 1608

I MUST depart, but like to his laſt breath
   That leaves the ſeat of life for liberty,
I go, but dying, and in this our death
Where ſoul and ſoul is parted, it is I
     The deader part yet fly away,
        While ſhe, alas! in whom before
        I liv'd, dies her own death and more,
     I feeling mine too much, and her own ſtay.
But ſince I muſt depart, and that our love
Springing at firſt but in an earthly mould
Tranſplanted to our ſouls, now doth remove
Earthly affects, which time and diſtance would,
     Nothing now can our loves allay,
        Though as the better Spirits will
        That both love us and know our ill,
     We do not either all the good we may.
Thus when our Souls that muſt immortal be,
   For our loves cannot die, nor we (unleſs
We die not both together) ſhall be free
   Unto their open and eternal peace.
Sleep, Death's Embaſſador, and beſt
   Image, doth yours often ſo ſhow,
     That I thereby muſt plainly know,
Death unto us muſt be freedom and reſt

May 1608

MADRIGAL.

How should I love my best?
 What though my love unto that height be grown,
  That taking joy in you alone,
  I utterly this world detest.
Should I not love it yet as th' only place,
 Where Beauty hath his perfect grace,
  And is possest?

  But I beauties despise
You, universal beauty seem to me,
 Giving and shewing form and degree
  To all the rest, in your fair eyes.
Yet should I not love them as parts whereon
 Your beauty, their perfection,
  And top doth rise?

  But ev'n my self I hate.
So far my love is from the least delight,
 That at my very self I spite.
  Senseless of any happy state,
Yet may I not with justest reason fear,
 How hating hers, I truly her
  Can celebrate?

Madrigal.

  Thus unresolved still,
Although world, life, nay what is fair beside,
  I cannot for your sake abide,
    Methinks I love not to my fill.
Yet, if a greater love you can devise,
  In loving you some otherwise,
    Believe't I will.

ANOTHER.

Dear, when I did from you remove,
   I left my joy, but not my love;
     That never can depart.
It neither higher can ascend,
     Nor lower bend.
Fixt in the centre of my heart,
     As in his place,
And lodged so, how can it change,
     Or you grow strange?
Those are earth's properties and base.
Each where, as the bodies divine,
   Heav'n's lights and you to me will shine.

TO HIS FRIEND BEN JOHNSON, OF HIS HORACE MADE ENGLISH.

IT was not enough Ben Johnson to be thought
   Of Englifh Poets beft, but to have brought
In greater ftate to their acquaintance one
So equal to himfelf and thee, that none
Might be thy fecond, while thy Glory is
To be the Horace of our times and his

EPITAPH. CÆCIL-BOULFER
QUÆ POST LANGUESCENTEM MORBUM
NON SINE INQUIETUDINE
SPIRITUS &c. CONSCIENTIÆ OBIIT

<small>Intelligitur de figurâ mortis præfigendâ.</small>

METHINKS Death like one laughing lies,
    Shewing his teeth, shutting his eyes,
Only thus to have found her here
He did with so much reason fear,
    And she despise.

For barring all the gates of Sin,
Death's open ways to enter in,
She was with a strict siege beset,
So what by force he could not get,
    By time to win.

This mighty Warrior was deceived yet,
For what he mutin* in her powers, thought
    Was but their zeal,
And what by their excess might have been wrought,
    Her fasts did heal.

---
* Mutiny

Epitaph Cæcil Boulfer.

Till that her noble soul, by these, as wings,
Transcending the low pitch of earthly things,
As being reliev'd by God and set at large,
And grown by this, worthy a higher charge,
Triumphing over Death to Heaven fled,
And did not die, but left her body dead

July 1609

EPITAPH GULI. HERBERT DE SWANSEY
QUI SINE PROLE OBIIT AUG. 1609

GREAT Spirit, that in New Ambition,
    Stoop'd not below his merit,
But with his proper worth being carry'd on,
Stoop'd at no second place, till now in one
    He doth all place inherit

Live endless here in such brave memory,
    The best tongue cannot spot it,
While they which knew, or but have heard of thee,
Must never hope thy like again to be,
    Since thou hast not begot it.

IN A GLASS WINDOW FOR INCONSTANCY.

LOVE, of this cleareſt, fraileſt glaſs,
    Divide the properties, ſo as
In the diviſion may appear
Clearneſs for me, frailty for her.

ELEGY FOR THE PRINCE.*

MUST he be ever dead? Cannot we add
    Another life unto that Prince that had
Our souls laid up in him? Could not our love,
Now when he left us, make that body move
After his death one Age? And keep unite
That frame wherein our souls did so delight?
For what are souls but love? since they do know
Only for it, and can no further go.
Sense is the Soul of Beasts, because none can
Proceed so far as t'understand like man
And if Souls be more where they love than where
They animate, why did it not appear
In keeping him alive? Or how is fate
Equal to us, when one man's private hate
May ruin Kingdoms, when he will expose
Himself to certain death, and yet all those
Not keep alive this Prince, who now is gone,
Whose loves would give thousands of lives for one?
Do we then die in him, only as we
May in the world's harmonique body see
An universally diffused soul

---

* Henry, Prince of Wales He died in November, 1612

Elegy for the Prince.

Move in the parts which moves not in the whole?
So though we rest with him, we do appear
To live and stir awhile, as if he were
Still quickening us? Or do (perchance) we live
And know it not? See we not Autumn give
Back to the earth again what it received
In th' early Spring? And may not we deceived
Think that those powers are dead, which do but sleep,
And the world's soul doth reunited keep?
And though this Autumn gave what never more
Any Spring can unto the world restore,
May we not be deceived, and think we know
Ourselves for dead? Because that we are so
Unto each other, when as yet we live
A life his love and memory doth give,
Who was our world's soul, and to whom we are
So reunite, that in him we repair
All other our affections ill bestowed
Since by this love we now have such abode
With him in Heaven as we had here, before
He left us dead Nor shall we question more
Whether the Soul of Man be memory
As Plato thought * We and posterity

---

* It would be interesting to know where Plato has made this singular assertion I fear it is more easy to account for Herbert's remark than to corroborate it

34

Elegy for the Prince.

Shall celebrate his name, and virtuous grow
Only in memory that he was so,
And on those terms we may seem yet to live,
Because he lived once, though we shall strive
To sigh away this seeming life so fast,
As if with us 'twere not already past.
We then are dead, for what doth now remain
To please us more, or what can we call pain
Now we have lost him? And what else doth make
Difference in life and death, but to partake
Nor Joy nor Pain? Oh death! could'st not fulfil
Thy rage against us no way but to kill
This Prince in whom we liv'd? that so we all
Might perish by thy hand at once, and fall
Under his ruin? Thenceforth though we should
Do all the actions that the living would,
Yet we shall not remember that we live,
No more than when our mother's womb did give
That life we felt not. Or should we proceed
To such a wonder, that the dead should breed,
It should be wrought to keep that memory
Which being his, can, therefore, never die.

November 9, 1612.

EPITAPH OF KING JAMES.

HERE lies King James, who did so propagate
    Unto the World that blest and quiet state
Wherein his subjects liv'd, he seemed to give
That peace which Christ did leave, and did so live,
As once that King and Shepherd of his Sheep,
That whom God saved, here he seemed to keep,
Till with that innocent and single heart
With which he first was crown'd he did depart,
To better life. Great Brittain, so lament
That Strangers more than thou may yet resent
The sad effects, and while they feel the harm
They must endure from the victorious arm
Of our King Charles, may they so long complain,
That tears in them force thee to weep again.

A VISION.
A LADY COMBING HER HAIR.

WITHIN an open curled fea of gold   The hair
   A Bark of Ivory one day I faw,   The comb.
  Which ftriking with his oars did feem to draw   The teeth of
Tow'rds a fair Coaft which I then did behold.   the comb.
                                                           Her fide.

A Lady held the Stern, while her white hand,
   Whiter than either ivory or sail,   The cuff or
  Over the furging waves did fo prevail   fmock fleeve
That fhe had now approached near the land.   Her fhoulder

When fuddenly, as if fhe feared fome wrack,
   And yet the Sky was fair, and Air was clear,
  And neither Rock, nor Monfter did appear   Wart
Doubling the Point, which fpied, fhe turned back

Then with a fecond courfe I faw her fteer,   Combing in an-
   As if fhe meant to reach fome other Bay,   other place
  Where being approached, fhe likewife turned away,
Though in the Bark fome waves now entred were.   Hairs in the
                                                           comb.

A Vision.

    Though varying oft her courſe at laſt I found,
        While I in queſt of the Adventure go,
<small>She had given over combing</small>   The Sail took down and Oars had ceas'd to row,
    And that the Bark itſelf was run aground.

<small>Her face</small>
    Wherewith Earth's faireſt creature I beheld,
        For which both Bark and Sea I gladly loſt.
<small>Her hair put up and comb caſt away</small>   Let no Philoſopher, of Knowledge boaſt,
    Unleſs that he my Viſion can unfold

TEARS flow no more, or if you needs must flow,
      Fall yet more flow,
    Do not the world invade.
From smaller springs than yours rivers have grown,
    And they again a Sea have made
Brackish like you, and which like you hath flown.

Ebb to my heart, and on the burning fires
      Of my desires
    Let your torrents fall.
From smaller Sparks than theirs such sparks arise
    As into flame converting all,
This world might be but my love's sacrifice.

Yet if, the tempests of my sighs, so slow
      You both must flow,
    And my desires still burn,
Since that in vain all help my love requires,
    Why may not yet their rages turn
To dry those tears and to blow out those fires?

Italy, 1614

DITTY

*TO THE TUNE OF A CHE DEL QUANTO MIO
OF PESARINO*

WHERE now shall these accents go?
    At which creatures silent grow
While Woods and Rocks do speak,
    And seem to break
Complains too long for them to hear,
Saying I call in vain   *Echo*—All in vain
   · =   . = ·   =
Where there is no relief. *Ec.*—Here is no relief.

Ah why then should I fear
Unto her rocky heart to speak that grief
In whose laments these bear a part?
    Then, cruel heart,
    Do but some answer give.
I do but crave. = Do you forbid to live or bid to live?
    Echo—Live

DITTY.

CAN I then live to draw that breath
    Which muſt bid farewell to thee?
Yet how ſhould death not ſeize on me?
Since abſence from the life I hold ſo dear muſt
    needs be death.

    While I do feel in parting
      Such a living dying,
    As in this my moſt fatal hour,
      Grief ſuch a life doth lend
    As quick'ned by his power
      Even death cannot end

I am the firſt that ever lov'd,
    He yet that for the place contends,
    Againſt true love ſo much offends
That even this way it is prov'd.

Ditty.

For whose affection once is shown,
   No longer can the World beguile,
   Who sees his penance all the while,
He holds a Torch to make her known.

You are the first were ever lov'd,
   And who may think this not so true,
   So little knows of love or you,
It need not otherwise be prov'd.

For though the more judicious eyes
   May know when Diamonds are right,
   There is required a greater light
Their estimate and worth to prize.

While they who most for beauty strive
   Can with no Art so lovely grow,
   As she who doth but only owe
So much as true affections give

Thus first of Lovers I appear,
   For more appearance makes me none,
   And thus are you belov'd alone,
That are priz'd infinitely dear

Epitaph of a Stinking Poet.

Yet, as in our Northern Clime,
    Rare fruits, though late, appear at laſt;
    As we may ſee ſome years being paſt,
Our Orange trees grow ripe with time.

So think not ſtrange, if Love to break
    His wonted Silence now makes bold;
    For a Love is ſeven years old,
Is it not time to learn to ſpeak?

Then gather in that, which doth grow
    And ripen to that faireſt hand
    'Tis not enough that trees do ſtand
If their fruit fall and periſh too.

EPITAPH OF A STINKING POET.

HERE ſtinks a Poet I confeſs,
    Yet wanting breath ſtinks ſo much leſs.

A DITTY TO THE TUNE OF COSE FERITE,

MADE BY LORENZO ALLEGRE TO ONE
SLEEPING   *To be sung.*

AH *Wonder!*
   So fair a heaven,
   So fair, &c.
And no Star shining
Ay me and no Star, &c
'Tis past my divining.

   Yet stay!
May not perchance this be some rising Morn
     Which in the scorn
Of our World's light discloses
This air of violets, that sky of roses?

   'Tis so!
An oriental sphere
Doth open and appear,
     Ascending bright;
Then since thy hymen I chant
May'st thou new pleasures grant,
     Admired light

EPITAPH

ON SIR EDWARD SACKVILLE'S CHILD,

WHO DIED IN HIS BIRTH.

READER! here lies a child that never cried,
    And therefore never died.
      'Twas neither old nor yong,
Born to this and the other world in one.
      Let us then ceaſe to moan,
Nothing that ever died hath liv'd ſo long

KISSING.

COME hither, Womankind, and all their worth,
    Give me thy kisses as I call them forth,
Give me thy billing kifs; that of the Dove,
    A Kifs of Love;
The Melting Kifs, a Kifs that doth confume
    To a perfume,
The extract Kifs, of every fweet a part,
    A Kifs of Art;
The Kifs which ever ftirs fome new delight,
    A Kifs of Might,
The twacking fmacking Kifs, and when you ceafe,
    A Kifs of Peace,
The Mufick Kifs, crotchet and quaver time,
    The Kifs of Rhyme,
The Kifs of Eloquence which doth belong
    Unto the tongue,
The Kifs of all the Sciences in one,
    The Kifs alone.
So 'tis enough

DITTY.

IF you refuse me once, and think again,
      I will complain.
You are deceived; Love is no work of Art,
    It must be got and born,
      Not made and worn,
Or such wherein you have no part.

Or do you think they more than once can die
      Whom you deny?
Who tell you of a thousand deaths a day,
    Like the old Poets feign,
      And tell the pain
They met but in the common way?

Or do you think it is too soon to yield
      And quit the Field?
You are deceived, they yield who first intreat
    Once one may crave for love,
      But more would prove
This heart too little, that too great

Ditty

Give me then so much love, that we may burn
  Past all return,
Who midst your beauties, flames, and spirit live,
  So great a light must find
   As to be blind
To all but what their fires give

Then give me so much love, as in one point,
  Fixed and conjoint,
May make us equal in our flames arise,
  As we shall never start,
   Until we dart
Lightning upon the envious eyes

Then give me so much love, that we may move
  Like stars of love,
And glad and happy times to Lovers bring,
  While glorious in one sphere
   We still appear
And keep an everlasting spring.

ELEGY OVER A TOMB.

MUST I then see, alas! eternal night
    Sitting upon those fairest eyes,
And closing all those beams, which once did rise
    So radiant and bright,
That light and heat in them to us did prove
    Knowledge and Love?

Oh, if you did delight no more to stay
    Upon this low and earthly stage,
But rather chose an endless heritage,
    Tell us at least, we pray,
Where all the beauties that those ashes ow'd
    Are now bestow'd?

Doth the Sun now his light with yours renew?
    Have Waves the curling of your hair?
Did you restore unto the Sky and Air
    The red and white and blue?
Have you vouchsafed to flowers since your death,
    That sweetest breath?

Elegy over a Tomb.

Had not Heav'n's Lights elfe in their houfes flept,
    Or to fome private life retir'd?
Muft not the Sky and Air have elfe confpir'd
    And in their Regions wept?
Muft not each flower elfe the earth could breed
    Have been a weed?

But thus enrich'd may we not yield fome caufe
    Why they themfelves lament no more,
That muft have changed courfe they held before,
    And broke their proper Laws,
Had not your Beauties giv'n their fecond birth
    To Heaven and Earth?

Tell us, for Oracles muft ftill afcend
    For thofe that crave them at your tomb;
Tell us, where are thofe Beauties now become
    And what they now intend;
Tell us, alas! that cannot tell our grief,
    Or hope relief.

1617.

EPITAPH ON SIR FRANCIS VERE.

READER,—
  If thou appear
 Before that tomb attention give,
  And do not fear,
  Unlefs it be to live,
For dead is great Sir Francis Vere.

Of whom this might be faid, Should God ordain
 One to deftroy all finners whom That One
 Redeem'd not there, that fo He might atone
His chofen flock, and take from earth that ftain
 That fpots it ftill, he worthy were alone
 To finifh it, and have, when they were gone,
This world for him made Paradife again.

TO MRS DIANA CECYLL

DIANA CECYLL, that rare beauty thou doſt
    ſhow
  Is not of Milk, or Snow,
Or ſuch as pale and whitely things do owe,
But an illuſtrious Oriental Bright,
  Like to the Diamond's refracted light,
Or early Morning breaking from the Night.

Nor are thy hair and eyes made of that ruddy beam
    Or golden-ſanded ſtream
  Which we find ſtill the vulgar Poet's theme,
But reverend black, and ſuch as you would ſay
Light did but ſerve it, and did ſhew the way
By which at firſt night did precede the day.

Nor is that ſymmetry of parts and form divine
    Made of one vulgar line,
  Or ſuch as any know how to define,
But of proportions new, ſo well expreſt
That the perfections in each part confeſt
Are beauties to themſelves and to the reſt.

To Mrs. Diana Cecyll.

Wonder of all thy Sex! let none henceforth inquire
    Why they so much admire,
  Since they that know thee best ascend no higher
Only be not with common praises wooed,
Since admiration were no longer good,
When men might hope more then they understood.

TO HER EYES.

BLACK eyes, if you seem dark,
    It is because your beams are deep
    And with your soul united keep
      Who could discern
Enough into them there, might learn
    Whence they derive that mark,
      And how their power is such
That all the wonders which proceed from thence,
Affecting more the mind then sense,
      Are not so much
The works of light, as influence.

    As you then joined are
Unto the soul, so it again
By its connexion doth pertain
    To that first cause,
Who, giving all their proper Laws,
    By you doth best declare
      How he at first being hid

To her Eyes.

Within the veil of an eternal night,
Did frame for us a second light,
    And after bid
It serve for ordinary sight

    His image then you are;
If there be any yet who doubt
What power it is that doth look out
    Through that your black,
He will not an example lack,
    If he suppose that there
    Were grey or hazel Glass,
And that through them, though sight or soul
    might shine,
He must yet at the last define
    That beams which pass
Through black, cannot but be divine.

TO HER HAIR.

BLACK beamy hairs, which so seem to arise
    From the extraction of those eyes,
That unto you she destin-like doth spin
The beams she spares, what time her soul retires,
      And by those hallowed fires
      Keeps house all night within

Since from within her awful front you shine,
    As threads of life which she doth twine,
And thence ascending with the fatal rays
To crown those temples, where Love's wonders
    wrought,
      We afterwards see brought
      To vulgar light and praise

Lighten through all your regions, till we find
    The causes why we are grown blind,
That when we should your Glories comprehend,
Our sight recoils, and turneth back again,
      And doth, as 'twere in vain,
      Itself to you extend

To her Hair.

Is it, becaufe paſt black, there is not found
    A fix'd or horizontal bound?
And ſo as it doth terminate the white,
It may be ſaid all colours to infold,
    And in that kind to hold
    Somewhat of infinite?

Or is it that the centre of our ſight,
    Being veiled in its proper night,
Diſcerns your blackneſs by ſome other ſenſe
Than that by which it doth pied colours ſee,
    Which only therefore be
    Known by their difference?

Tell us, when on her front in curls you lie,
    So diaper'd from that black eye,
That your reflected forms may make us know
That ſhining light in darkneſs all would find,
    Were they not upward blind
    With the Sun-beams below.

SONNET OF BLACK BEAUTY.

BLACK beauty, which above that common light,
 Whose Power can no colors here renew
But those which darkness can again subdue,
Dost still remain unvary'd to the light?

And like an object equal to the view,
 And neither chang'd with day nor hid with night,
 When all these colours which the world call bright,
And which old Poetry doth so pursue,

Are with the night so perished and gone,
 That of their being there remains no mark,
Thou still abidest so entirely one,
 That we may know thy blackness is a spark
Of light inaccessible, and alone
 Our darkness which can make us think it dark

ANOTHER SONNET TO BLACK IT SELF.

THOU Black wherein all colours are compos'd,
    And unto which they all at last return;
Thou colour of the Sun where it both burn,
And shadow, where it cools; in thee is clos'd
Whatever nature can, or hath dispos'd
    In any other here; from thee do rise
Those tempers and complexions which disclos'd
    As parts of thee, do work as mysteries
Of that thy hidden power, when thou dost reign
    The characters of fate shine in the Skies,
And tell us what the Heavens do ordain:
    But when Earth's common light shines to our eyes
Thou so retir'st thyself, that thy disdain
    All revelation unto man denies.

THE FIRST MEETING.

AS sometimes with a Sable Cloud
    We see the Heavns bow'd,
And darkning all the fire,
Until the lab'ring fires they do contain
    Break forth again,
Ev'n so from under your black hair
  I saw such an unusual blaze
Lightning and sparkling from your eyes,
And with unused prodigies
    Forcing such amaze,
That I did judge your empire here
Was not of love alone but fear

But as all that is violent
Doth by degrees relent;
So when that sweetest face,
Growing at last to be serene and clear,
    Did now appear
With all its wonted heav'nly grace,

The First Meeting.

And your appeafed eyes did send
A beam from them fo foft and mild
That former terrors were exil'd,
And all that could amaze did end;
Darknefs in me was chang'd to light,
Wonder to love, love to delight.

Nor here yet did your goodnefs ceafe
My heart and eyes to blefs,
   For, being paft all hope
That I could now enjoy a better ftate,
     An orient gate
(As if the Heav'ns themfelves did ope)
Firft found in thee, and then difclof'd
   So gracious and fweet a fmile,
That my foul ravifhed the while,
And wholly from itfelf unloof'd,
Seem'd hov'ring in your breath to rife
To feel an air of Paradife.

Nor here yet did your favours end,
For whilft I down did bend,
As one who now did mifs
A foul which grown much happier than before
   Would turn no more,
You did beftow on me a kifs,

The First Meeting.

And in that kifs a foul infufe
Which was fo fafhion'd by your mind,
And which was fo much more refin'd
   Than that I formerly did ufe,
That if one foul found joys in thee,
The other framed them new in me.

But as thofe bodies which difpenfe
Their beams, in parting hence
Thofe beams do recollect,
Until they in themfelves refumed have
     The forms they gave,
So when your gracious afpect
  From me was turned once away,
Neither could I thy foul retain
Nor you give mine leave to remain,
  To make with you a longer ftay,
Or fuffered ought elfe to appear
But your hair, night's hemifphere.

Only as we in Loadftones find
Virtue of fuch a kind,
That what they once do give,
Being neither to be chang'd by any Clime
    Or forc'd by time,
Doth ever in its fubjects live,

The First Meeting.

So though I be from you retir'd,
The power you gave yet still abides,
And my soul ever so guides
By your magnetique touch inspir'd,
That all it moves, or is inclin'd,
Comes from the motions of your mind

A MERRY RIME

SENT TO THE LADY WROTH UPON THE BIRTH OF MY LORD OF PEMBROKE'S CHILD, BORN IN THE SPRING.

MADAM, though I'm one of thofe,
    That every fpring ufe to compofe,
That is, add feet unto round profe,
Yet you a further art difclofe,
And can, as every body knows,
Add to thofe feet fine dainty toes
Satyrs add nails, but they are fhrews.
My mufe therefore no further goes,
But for her feet craves fhooes and hofe,
Let a fair feafon add a Rofe.
While thus attir'd we'll oppofe
The tragick bufkins of our foes.
And herewith, Madam, I will clofe,
And 'tis no matter how it fhows:
All I care is, if the Child grows.

THE THOUGHT.

IF you do love as well as I,
    Then every minute from your heart
        A thought doth part,
And winged with defire doth fly
Till it hath met in a ftreight line
        A thought of mine,
So like to yours, we cannot know
Whether of both doth come or go,
        Till we define
Which of us two that thought did owe.

I say then that your thoughts which pafs
Are not fo much the thoughts you meant
        As thofe I fent,
For as my image in a glafs
Belongs not to the glafs you fee,
        But unto me,
So when your fancy is fo clear
That you would think you faw me there,
        It needs muft be
That it was I did firft appear.

The Thought.

Likewise when I send forth a thought
My reason tells me, 'tis the same
  Which from you came,
And which your beauteous Image wrought.
Thus while our thoughts by turns do lead
  None can precede ,
And thus while in each other's mind
Such interchanged forms we find,
  Our loves may plead
To be of more then vulgar kind.

May you then often think on me,
And by that thinking know 'tis true
  I thought on you.
I in the same belief will be,
While by this mutual address
  We will possess
A love must live, when we do die.
Which rare and secret property
  You will confess,
If you do love as well as I.

TO A LADY WHO DID SING EXCELLENTLY.

WHEN our rude and unfashioned words, that long
A being in their elements enjoy'd,
  Senseless and void,
Come at last to be formed by thy tongue,
And from thy breath receive that life and place,
  And perfect grace,
That now thy power, diffus'd through all their parts,
  Are able to remove
All the obstructions of the hardest hearts,
And teach the most unwilling how to love.

When they again, exalted by thy voice,
Tun'd by thy soul, dismiss'd into the air,
  To us repair,
A living, moving, and harmonious noise,
Able to give the love they do create
  A second state,

To a Lady who did Sing excellently.

And charm not only all his griefs away,
   And his defects restore,
But make him perfect, who, the Poets say,
Made all was ever yet made heretofore

When again all these rare perfections meet,
Composed in the circle of thy face,
   As in their place,
So to make up of all one perfect sweet,
Who is not then so ravished with delight,
   Ev'n of thy sight,
That he can be assur'd his sense is true,
   Or that he die, or live,
Or that he do enjoy himself, or you,
Or only the delights, which you did give?

MELANDER,
SUPPOS'D TO LOVE SUSAN, BUT DID LOVE ANN.

WHO doth presume my Mistress's name to scan
  Goes about more than any way he can,
Since all men think that it is *Susan*.   *Echo*—Anne.

What sayst?   Then tell who is as white as Swan,
While others set by her are pale and wan;
Then, Echo, speak, Is it not *Susan*?   *Ec.*—Anne.

Tell, Echo, yet, who's Middle's but a span,
Some being gross as bucket, round as pan?
Say, Echo, then, Is it not *Susan*?   *Ec.*—Anne.

Say, is she not soft as meal without bran?
Though yet in great haste once from me she ran,
Must I not however love *Susan*?   *Ec.*—Anne.

ECHO TO A ROCK.

THOU heaven-threatening Rock, gentler then she,
  Since of my pain
 Thou still more sensible will be,
Only when thou giv'st leave but to complain.
   Echo—Complain.
But thou dost answer too, although in vain
Thou answer'st when thou can'st no pity show
   Echo—Oh!
 What, canst thou speak and pity too?
 Then yet a further favour do,
And tell if of my griefs I any end shall know.
   Echo—No.
Sure she will pity him that loves her so truly.
   Echo—You lie.
Vile Rock, thou now grow'st so unruly,
That hadst thou life, as thou hast voice,
 Thou shouldst die at my foot.
    Echo—Die at my foot.

Echo to a Rock.

Thou canſt not make me do't
Unleſs thou leave it to my choice,
Who thy hard ſentence ſhall fulfill,
When thou ſhalt ſay I die to pleaſe her only will
   Echo—I will.
When ſhe comes hither, then, I pray thee, tell
Thou art my Monument, and this my laſt farewell.
   Echo—Well.

ECHO IN A CHURCH.

WHEN shall my troubled soul at large
    Discharge
The burden of her sins, oh where?
    Echo—Here
Whence comes this voice I hear?
  Who doth this grace afford?
If it be thou, O Lord,

Say if thou hear my prayers, when I call.
    Echo—All
And wilt thou pity grant when I do cry?
    Echo—I

Then though I fall,
  Thy grace will my defects supply
  But who will keep my soul from ill,
Quench bad desires, reform my Will?
    Echo—I will.

O may that Will and Voice be bleſt
Which yields ſuch comforts unto one diſtreſt !
More bleſſed yet, would'ſt thou thyſelf unmaſk,
Or tell at leaſt who undertakes this taſk
   Echo—Aſk.

Since now with crying I am grown ſo weak,
I ſhall want force even to crave thy name.
O ſpeak before I wholly weary am.
   Echo—I am.

TO HIS MISTRESS FOR HER TRUE PICTURE.

DEATH, my life's Mistress, and the Sovereign Queen
Of all that ever breath'd, though yet unseen,
My heart doth love you best, yet I confess,
Your picture I beheld, which doth express
No such eye-taking beauty, you seem lean,
Unless you're mended since. Sure he did mean
No honour to you, that did draw you so,
Therefore I think it false. Besides, I know
The picture Nature drew (which sure's the best)
Doth figure you by sleep and sweetest rest.
Sleep, Nurse of our life, Care's best reposer,
Nature's high'st rapture, and the vision giver.
Sleep, which when it doth seize us, souls go play,
And make Man equal as he was first day.
Yet some will say can pictures have more life
Than the original? To end this strife,
Sweet Mistress come, and shew yourself to me
In your true form, while then I think to see
Some beauty Angelick, that comes to unlock
My body's prison, and from life unfrock

To his Mistress for her true Picture.

My well-divorced Soul, and set it free
To liberty eternal: thus you see,
I find the Painter's error, and protect
Your absent Beauties, ill drawn, by th' effect
For grant it were your work and not the Grave's,
Draw Love by Madness then, Tyrants by Slaves,
Because they make men such. Dear Mistress, then,
If you would not be seen by owl-ey'd men,
Appear at noon i'th' Air, with so much light
The Sun may be a Moon, the Day a Night,
Clear to my soul, but dark'ning the weak sense
Of those, the other World's Cimmeriens,
And in your fatal robe embroidered
With Star characters, teaching me to read
The destiny of Mortals, while your clear brow
Presents a Majesty, to instruct me how
To love, or dread nought else · May your bright hair,
Which are the threads of life, fair crown'd appear,
With that your Crown of Immortality.
In your right hand, the Keys of Heaven be,
In th' other, those of the Infernal Pit,
Whence none retires if once he enter it.
And here let me complain, how few are those
Whose souls you shall from earth's vast dungeon loose
To endless happiness, few that attend
You the true guide unto their journey's end

To his Mistress for her true Picture.

And if old Virtue's way narrow were,
'Tis rugged now, having no paſſenger
Our life is but a dark and ſtormy night,
To which ſenſe yields a weak and glimmering light,
While wandering Man thinks he diſcerneth all
By that which makes him but miſtake and fall.
He ſees enough, who doth his darkneſs ſee
Theſe are great lights, by which leſs dark'ned be
Shine then Sun-bright, or through my ſenſes' veil,
A day ſtar of the light doth never fail
Shew me that goodneſs which compounds the ſtrife
'Twixt a long ſickneſs and a weary life,
Set forth that Juſtice which keeps all in awe
Certain and equal more than any Law;
Figure that happy and eternal Reſt,
Which till man do enjoy, he is not bleſt,
Come and appear then, dear Soul-raviſher,
Heav'ns lighteſt Uſher, Man's deliverer,
And do not think, when I new beauties ſee,
They can withdraw my ſettled love from thee.
Fleſh-beauty ſtrikes me not at all, I know
When thou do'ſt leave them to the grave, they ſhow
Worſe than they now ſhow thee they ſhall not move
In me the leaſt part of delight, or love,
But as they teach your power   Be the nut brown,
The lovelieſt colour which the fleſh doth crown,

To his Mistress for her true Picture.

I'll think it like a Nut—a fair outside,
Within which worms and rottenness abide;
If fair, then like the Worm itself to be;
If painted, like their slime and fluttery.
If any yet will think their beauties best,
And will against you, spite of all, contest,
Seize them with Age; so in themselves they'll hate
What they scorn'd in your picture, and too late
See their fault, and the Painter's   Yet if this,
Which their great'st plague and wrinkled torture is,
Please not, you may to the more wicked sort,
Or such as of your praises make a sport,
Denounce an open war, send chosen bands
Of Worms, your soldiers, to their fairest hands,
And make them leprous, scabb'd . upon their face
Let those your Pioneers, Ringworms, take their place,
And safely near with strong approaches got,
Intrench it round, while their teeths' rampire rot,
With other Worms, nay with a damp inbred,
Sink to their senses, which they shall not dread.
And thus may all that ere they prided in,
Confound them now.   As for the parts within
Send great Worms, which may undermine a way
Into their vital parts, and so display
That, your pale ensign on the walls, then let
Those worms your Veterans which never yet

To his Mistress for her true Picture.

Did fail, enter pell-mell and ransack all.
Just as they see the well-rais'd building fall.
While they do this, your Forragers command,
The Caterpillars, to devour their land,
And with them Wasps, your wing'd-worm-horsemen, bring
To charge, in troop, those Rebels, with their sting.
All this, unless your beauty they confess.

And now, sweet Mistress, let me awhile digress
To admire these noble Worms whom I invoke,
And not the Muses. You that eat through oak
And bark, will you spare Paper and my Verse,
Because your praises they do here rehearse?

Brave Legions then, sprung from the mighty race
Of man corrupted, and which hold the place
Of his undoubted issue: you that are
Brain-born, Minerva-like, and, like her, war,
Well arm'd, complete, mail'd-jointed soldiers,
Whose force Herculean links in pieces tears,
To you the vengeance of all Spill-bloods falls,
Beast-eating Men, Men-eating cannibals,
Death privileg'd, were you in sunder smit,
You do not lose your life, but double it.
Best-framed types of the Immortal Soul,
Which in your selves, and in each part, are whole

To his Mistress for her true Picture.

Last-living Creatures, heirs of all the earth,
For when all men are dead, it is your birth;
When you die, your brave self-killed General,
For nothing else can kill him, doth end all.
What vermine-breeding body then thinks scorn
His flesh should be by your brave fury torn?
Willing, to you, this carcass I submit,
A gift so free, I do not care for it,
Which yet you shall not take until I see
My Mistress first reveal herself to me

Meanwhile, Great Mistress, whom my soul admires,
Grant me your true picture, who it desires,
That he your matchless beauty might maintain,
'Gainst all men that will quarrels entertain.
For a Flesh-Mistress, the worst I can do
Is but to keep the way that leads to you,
And howsoever the event doth prove,
To have Revenge below, Reward above.
Hear, from my body's prison, this my call,
Who from my mouth-grate and eye-window bawl

EPITAPH ON SIR PHILIP SIDNEY,

LYING IN ST PAUL'S WITHOUT A MONUMENT, TO BE FASTENED UPON THE CHURCH DOOR.

READER,—
    Within this church Sir Philip Sidney lies,
Nor is it fit that I should more acquaint,
      Lest Superstition rise,
      And men adore,
Soldiers, their Martyr, Lovers, their Saint

EPITAPH FOR HIMSELF.

READER,—
   The Monument which thou beholdeſt here,
     Preſents Edward Lord Herbert to thy ſight,
   A man, who was ſo free from either hope or fear,
     To have, or loſe this ordinary light,
   That when to elements his body turned were
     He knew, that as thoſe elements would fight,
   So his Immortal Soul ſhould find above
   With his Creator, Peace, Joy, Faith, and Love

SONNET.

YOU well-compacted groves, whose light and shade
    Mixt equally, produce nor heat nor cold,
Either to burn the young, or freeze the old,
But to one even temper being made,
Upon a Grove embroidering through each glade
An Airy Silver, and a Sunny Gold,
So clothe the poorest that they do behold
Themselves in riches which can never fade,
While the wind whistles, and the birds do sing,
While your twigs clip, and while the leaves do fuss,
While the fruit ripens which those trunks do bring,
Senseless to all but love, do you not spring
Pleasure of such a kind, as truly is
A self renewing vegetable bliss ?

Made upon the Groves near Merlou Castle.

TO THE C. OF D.*

SINCE in your face, as in a beauteous sphere,
    Delight and state so sweetly mix'd appear,
That Love's not light, nor Gravity severe,
All your attractive graces seem to draw,
A modest rigor keepeth so in awe,
That in their turns, each of them gives the law.

Therefore, though chaste and virtuous, desire
Through that, your native mildness, may aspire,
Until a just regard it dost acquire,
Yet if Love thence a forward hope project
You can, by virtue of a sweet neglect,
Convert it streight to reverend respect

Thus, as in your rare temper, we may find
An excellence so perfect in each kind,
That a fair body hath a fairer mind;
So all the beams you diversly do dart,
As well on th'understanding as the heart,
Of love and honour equal cause impart.

---

* Possibly the Countess of Denbigh, the patroness of Carew.

DITTY.

1.

WHY doſt thou hate return inſtead of love?
    And with ſuch mercileſs deſpite
      My faith and hope requite?
    Oh! if th' affection cannot move,
    Learn innocence yet of the Dove,
And thy diſdain to juſter bounds confine.
Or if t'wards Man thou equally decline
The rules of Juſtice and of Mercy too,
Thou may'ſt thy love to ſuch a point refine
As it will kill more than thy hate can do.

2.

Love, love, Melaina, then, though death enſue,
    Yet it is a greater fate
    To die through love than hate.
    Rather a victory purſue
    To Beauty's lawful conqueſt due,

Ditty.

Than tyrant eyes envenom with disdain.
Or if thy Power thou wouldst so maintain
As equally to be both lov'd and dread,
Let timely Kisses call to life again
Him whom thine eyes have Planet-strucken dead

3.

Kiss, kiss, Melaina, then, and do not stay
    Until these sad effects appear
    Which now draw on so near,
    That didst thou longer help delay
    My soul must fly so fast away
As would at once both life and love divorce;
Or if I needs must die without remorse,
Kiss and embalm me so with that sweet breath,
That while thou triumph'st o'er Love and his force,
I may triumph yet over Fate and Death.

ELEGY FOR DOCTOR DUNN.*

WHAT though the vulgar and received praise
With which each common Poet strives to raise
His worthless Patron, seem to give the height
Of a true excellence, yet as the weight
Forced from his centre, must again recoil,
So every praise, as if it took some foil
Only because it was not well imploy'd,
Turns to those senseless principles and void,
Which in some broken syllables being vouched
Cannot above an Alphabet be couched,
In which dissolved state they used to rest
Until some other in new forms invest
Their easy matter, striving so to fix
Glory with words and make the parts to mix.

But since praise that wants truth, like words that want
Their proper meaning, doth it self recant,
Such terms, however elevate and high,
Are but like meteors, which the pregnant Sky

---

* He will be better recognised as Dr. John Donne. He died March 31st, 1631

Elegy for Dr. Dunn.

Varies in divers figures, till at laſt
They either be by ſome dark cloud o'recaſt,
Or wanting inward ſuſtence do devolve,
And into their firſt Elements reſolve.
Praiſes, like garments then, if looſe and wide,
Are ſubject to fall off; if gay and pied,
Make men ridiculous: The juſt and grave
Are thoſe alone which men may wear and have.

How fitting were it then each had that part
Which is their due, and that no fraudulent art
Could ſo diſguiſe the truth but they might own
Their rights, and by that property be known.
For ſince Praiſe is publick inheritance,
If any Inter-Commoner do chance
To give or take more praiſe than doth belong
Unto his part, he doth ſo great a wrong,
That all who claim an equal intereſt
May him implead until he do deveſt
His uſurpations, and again reſtore
Unto the Publick what was theirs before.

Praiſes ſhould then, like definitions, be
Round, neat, convertible, ſuch as agree
To perſons, ſo that were their names conceal'd
Muſt make them known as well as if reveal'd,

Elegy for Dr. Dunn.

Such as contain the kind and difference
And all the properties arising thence.
All praises else, as more or less than due,
Will prove, or strangly false, or weakly true.

Having delivered now what praises are,
It rests that I should to the world declare
Thy praises, DUNN, whom I so lov'd alive
That with my witty Carew I should strive
To celebrate the dead, did I not need
A language by itself, which should exceed
All those which are in use: For while I take
Those common words, which men may even rake
From Dunghill-wits, I find them so defiled,
Slubber'd and false, as if they had exiled
Truth and propriety, such as do tell
So little other things, they hardly spell
Their proper meaning, and therefore unfit
To blazon forth thy merits, or thy wit.

Nor will it serve that thou didst so refine
Matter with words that both did seem divine
When thy breath utter'd them, for thou being gone
They streight did follow thee. Let therefore none
Hope to find out an Idiom and Sense
Equal to thee and to thy Eminence,

Elegy for Dr. Dunn.

Unless our gracious King give words their bound,
Call in false titles which each where are found
In Prose and Verse, and as bad Coin and Light
Suppress them and their values, till the right
Take place and do appear, and then in lieu
Of those forg'd Attributes stamp some anew,
Which being current and by all allow'd
In Epitaphs and Tombs might be avow'd
More then their Escucheons.   Meanwhile, because
Nor praise is yet confined to its laws,
Nor railing wants his proper dialect,
Let thy detraction thy late life detect,
And though they term all thy heat, forwardness,
Thy solitude, self-pride, fasts, niggardness,
And on this false supposal would infer
They teach not others right, themselves who err,
Yet as men to the adverse part do ply
Those crooked things, which they would rectify,
So would perchance to loose and wanton Man
Such vice avail more than their virtues can.

THE BROWN BEAUTY.

1.

WHILE the two contraries of Black and White,
   In the Brown Fay are so well unite,
That they no longer now seem opposite,
Who doubts but love hath this his colour chose,
Since he therein doth both th'extremes compose,
And as within their proper Centre close?

2.

Therefore, as it presents not to the view
That whitely raw and unconcocted hue
Which, Beauty, Northern Nations think the true,
So neither hath it that adust aspect
The Moor and Indian so much affect,
That for it they all other do reject.

3.

Thus while the White well shadow'd doth appear,
And black doth through his lustre grow so clear
That each in other equal part doth bear,

The Brown Beauty.

All in so rare proportion is combin'd
That the fair temper, which adorns her mind,
Is even to her outward form confin'd.

4.

Fay, your sexe's honour, then so live
That when the world shall with contention strive
To whom they would a chief perfection give,
They might the controversy so decide
As, quitting all extremes on either side,
You more than any may be dignify'd.

AN ODE

UPON A QUESTION MOVED WHETHER LOVE SHOULD CONTINUE FOR EVER

HAVING interr'd her Infant-birth,
    The wat'ry ground, that late did mourn
    Was strew'd with flow'rs, for the return
    Of the wish'd Bridegroom of the Earth.

The well-accorded Birds did sing
    Their hymns unto the pleasant time,
    And in a sweet consorted chime
Did welcome in the cheerful Spring.

To which, soft whistles of the Wind,
    And warbling murmurs of a Brook,
    And varied notes of leaves that shook,
An harmony of parts did bind.

While doubling joy unto each other
    All in so rare consent was shown,
    No happiness that came alone,
Nor pleasure that was not another.

An Ode.

When with a love none can expreſs
   That mutually happy pair,
   Melander and Celinda fair,
The ſeaſon with their loves did bleſs.

Walking thus towards a pleaſant grove,
   Which did, it ſeem'd, in new delight
   The pleaſures of the time unite,
They give a triumph to their love.

They ſtay'd at laſt and on the graſs
   Repoſed ſo, as o're his breaſt
   She bow'd her gracious head to reſt,
Such a weight as no burden was.

While over either's compaſs'd waiſt
   Their folded arms were ſo compoſ'd
   As if in ſtraiteſt bonds incloſ'd,
They ſuffer'd for joys they did taſte

Long their fixt eyes to Heaven bent,
   Unchanged they did never move,
   As if ſo great and pure a love
No glaſs but it could repreſent

When, with a ſweet though troubled look,
   She firſt brake ſilence, ſaying, Dear Friend,
   O that our love might take no end,
Or never had beginning took !

An Ode.

I speak not this with a false heart
   (Wherewith his hand she gently strain'd),
   Or that would change a love maintain'd
With so much faith on either part;

Nay, I protest, though Death with his
   Worst Counsel should divide us here,
   His terrors could not make me fear
To come where your lov'd presence is

Only, if love's fire with the breath
   Of life be kindled, I doubt
   With our last air 'twill be breath'd out,
And quenched with the cold of death;

That if affection be a line
   Which is clos'd up in our last hour,
   Oh, how 'twould grieve me, any pow'r
Could force so dear a love as mine!

She scarce had done, when his shut eyes
   An inward joy did represent
   To hear Celinda thus intent
To a love he so much did prize,

Then with a look, it seem'd deny'd
   All earthly pow'r but hers, yet so
   As if to her breath he did owe
This borrow'd life, he thus replied

An Ode.

O you, wherein, they say, Souls rest
   Till they descend, pure heavenly fires,
   Shall lustful and corrupt desires
With your immortal seed be blest?

And shall our Love, so far beyond
   That low and dying appetite,
   And which so chast desires unite,
Not hold in an eternal bond?

It is, because we should decline,
   And wholly from our thoughts exclude
   Objects that may the sense delude
And study only the Divine

No sure, for if none can ascend
   Ev'n to the visible degree
   Of things created, how should we
The invisible comprehend?

Or rather, since that Pow'r exprest
   His greatness in his works alone,
   Being here best in's Creatures known,
Why is he not lov'd in them best?

But is't not true, which you pretend,
   That since our love and knowledge here,
   Only as parts of life appear,
So they with it should take their end?

An Ode.

O no, Belov'd, I am most sure
   Those vertuous habits we acquire
   As being with the Soul entire
Must with it evermore endure,

For if, where sins and vice reside
   We find so foul a guilt remain,
   As never dying in his stain
Still punish'd in the Soul doth bide,

Much more that true and real joy,
   Which in a virtuous love is found
   Must be more solid in its ground
Then Fate or Death can e're destroy.

Else should our Souls in vain elect,
   And vainer yet were Heaven's laws,
   When to an everlasting Cause
They gave a perishing effect.

Nor here on earth then, or above,
   Our good affection can impair,
   For where God doth admit the fair
Think you that he excludeth Love?

These eyes again then eyes shall see,
   And hands again these hands enfold,
   And all chaste pleasures can be told
Shall with us everlasting be.

An Ode.

For if no use of sense remain,
    When bodies once this life forsake,
    Or they could no delight partake,
Why should they ever rise again?

And if every imperfect mind
    Make love the end of knowledge here,
    How perfect will our love be, where
All imperfection is refined!

Let then no doubt, Celinda, touch,
    Much less your fairest mind invade:
    Were not our souls immortal made
Our equal loves can make them such.

So when one wing can make no way
    Two joined can themselves dilate,
    So can two persons propagate
When singly either would decay.

So when from hence we shall be gone,
    And be no more, nor you, nor I,
    As one another's mystery,
Each shall be both, yet both but one

This said, in her uplifted face,
    Her eyes, which did that beauty crown,
    Were like two stars, that having fall'n down,
Look up again to find their place.

An Ode.

While such a moveless silent peace
    Did cease on their becalmed sense,
    One would have thought some Influence
Their ravish'd spirits did possess.

THE GREEN-SICKNESS BEAUTY.

THOUGH the pale white within your cheeks compos'd,
And doubtful light unto your eye confin'd,
Though your short breath not from it self unloos'd,
And careless motions of your equal mind,
Argue your beauties are not all disclos'd,

Yet as a rising beam, when first 'tis shewn,
Points fairer, than when it ascends more red,
Or as a budding rose, when first 'tis blown,
Smells sweeter far, than when it is more spread,
As all things best by principles are known,

So in your green and flourishing estate
A beauty is discern'd more worthy love
Than that which further doth itself dilate,
And those degrees of variation prove,
Our vulgar wits so much do celebrate.

The Green-Sickness Beauty.

Thus though your eyes dart not that piercing blaze,
Which doth in busy Lovers' looks appear,
It is because you do not need to gaze
On other objects than your proper sphere,
Nor wander further than to run that maze

So, if you want that blood which must succeed,
And give at last a tincture to your skin,
It is, because neither in outward deed,
Nor inward thought, you yet admit that sin,
For which your cheeks a guilty blush should need.

So if your breath do not so freely flow,
It is because you love not to consume
That vital treasure, which you do bestow
As well to vegetate as to perfume
Your Virgin leaves, as fast as they do grow

Yet stay not here   Love for his right will call.
You were not born to serve your only will,
Nor can your beauty be perpetual.
'Tis your perfection for to ripen still,
And to be gathered, rather than to fall.

THE GREEN-SICKNESS BEAUTY.

FROM thy pale look, while angry Love doth seem
    With more imperiousness to give his Law
Than when he blushingly doth beg esteem,
    We may observe pied beauty in such awe,
That the brav'st colour under her command
    Affrighted, oft before you doth retire,
While, like a Statue of your self, you stand
    In such symmetrique form, as doth require
No lustre but his own : As then in vain
    One should flesh-colouring to statues add,
So were it to your native White a Stain,
    If it in other ornaments were clad,
Than what your rich proportions do give,
    Which in a boundless fair being unconfin'd,
Exalted in your soul, so seem to live,
    That they become an emblem of your mind,
That so, who to your Orient White should join
    Those fading qualities most eyes adore,
Were but like one, who gilding Silver Coin,
    Gave but occasion to suspect it more.

LA GRALLETTA GALLANTE,

OR

THE SUN-BURN'D EXOTIQUE BEAUTY.

1.

CHILD of the Sun, in whom his Rays appear
    Hatch'd to that luftre, as doth make thee wear
Heav'n's livery in thy fkin, what need'ft thou fear
The injury of Air, and change of Clime,
When thy exalted form is fo fublime
As to tranfcend all power of change or time?

2.

How proud are they that in their hair but fhow
Some part of thee, thinking therein they owe
The greateft beauty Nature can beftow,
When thou art fo much fairer to the fight,
As beams each where diffufed are more bright
Than their deriv'd and fecondary light.

La Gralletta Gallante.

3.

But Thou art cordial both to fight and tafte,
While each rare fruit feems in his time to hafte
To ripen in thee, till at length they wafte
Themfelves to inward fweets, from whence again,
They, like Elixirs, paffing through each vein,
An endlefs circulation do maintain.

4.

How poor are they then, whom if we but greet,
Think that raw juice, which in their lips we meet,
Enough to make us hold their Kiffes fweet;
When that rich odour, which in thee is fmelt,
Can it felf to a balmy liquor melt,
And make it to our inward fenfes felt.

5.

Leave then thy Country, Soil, and Mother's Home,
Wander a Planet this way, till thou come
To give our Lovers here their fatal doom,
While, if our beauties fcorn to envy thine,
It will be juft they to a Jaundice pine,
And by thy Gold, fhow like fome Copper-Mine.

PLATONICK LOVE.

1

MADAM, your beauty and your lovely parts
   Would scarce admit poetic praise and arts,
As they are Love's most sharp and piercing darts;
Though, as again they only wound and kill,
The more deprav'd affections of our will,
You claim a right to commendation still.

2.

For as you can unto that height refine
All Loves delights, as while they do incline
Unto no vice, they so become divine,
We may as well attain your excellence,
As, without help of any outward sense
Would make us grow a pure Intelligence.

3

And as a Soul, thus being quite abstract,
Complies not properly with any act,
Which from its better Being may detract,
So, through the virtuous habits which you infuse
It is enough that we may like and choose,
Without presuming yet to take or use.

4.

Thus Angels in their starry Orbs proceed
Unto Affection, without other need
Than that they still on contemplation feed,
Though as they may unto this Orb descend,
You can, when you would so much lower bend,
Give Joys beyond what Man can comprehend.

5.

Do not refuse, then Madam, to appear,
Since every radiant Beam comes from your Sphere,
Can so much more than any else endear,
As while through them we do discern each Grace
The multiplied lights from every Place,
Will turn and circle, with their rays, your face.

PLATONICK LOVE.

1

MADAM, believe't, Love is not such a toy,
   As it is sport but for the Idle Boy,
Or wanton Youth, since it can entertain
Our serious thoughts, and make us know how vain
All time is spent we do not thus imploy.

2.

For though strong passion oft on youth doth seize
It is not yet affection, but disease,
Caused from repletion, which their blood doth vex,
So that they love not Woman, but the Sex,
And care no more than how themselves to please

3.

Whereas true Lovers check that appetite
Which would presume further than to invite
The Soul unto that part it ought to take,
When that from this address it would but make
Some introduction only to delight.

Platonick Love.

4
For while they from the outward sense transplant
The love grew there in earthly mould, and scant,
To the Soul's spacious and immortal field,
They spring a love eternal, which will yield
All that a pure affection can grant.

5
Besides, what time or distance might effect
Is thus remov'd, while they themselves connect
So far above all change, as to exclude
Not only all which might their sense delude,
But mind to any object else effect.

6.
Nor will the proof of Constancy be hard
When they have plac'd upon their Mind that guard
As no ignoble thought can enter there,
And Love doth such a Virtue persevere,
And in it self so find a just reward.

7.
And thus a love, made from a worthy choice,
Will to that union come, as but one voice,
Shall speak, one thought but think the other's will,
And while, but frailty, they can know no ill,
Their souls more than their bodies must rejoice

Platonick Love.

8

In which estate nothing can so fulfill
Those heights of pleasure, which their souls instill
Unto each other, but that love thence draws
New Arguments of joy, while the same cause
That makes them happy, makes them greater still.

9

So that however multiplied and vast
Their love increase, they will not think it past
The bounds of growth, till their exalted fire
Being equally inlarg'd with their desire,
Transform and fix them to one Star at last.

10.

Or when that otherwise they were inclin'd
Unto those publick joys, which are assign'd
To blessed Souls when they depart from hence,
They would, besides what Heaven doth dispense,
Have their contents they in each other find.

THE IDEA,

MADE OF ALNWICK IN HIS EXPEDITION TO SCOTLAND WITH THE ARMY, 1639.

ALL Beauties vulgar eyes on earth do see,
   At best but some Imperfect Copies be
Of those the Heavens did at first decree;

For though th' Ideas of each sev'ral kind
Conceiv'd above by the Eternal Mind
Are such, as none can error in them find,

Since from his thoughts and presence he doth bar
And shut out all deformity so far,
That the least beauty near him is a Star.

As Nature yet from far th' Ideas views,
And doth besides but vile materials choose,
We in her works observe no small abuse.

Some of her figures therefore soil'd and blurr'd,
Show as if Heaven had no way concurr'd
In shapes so disproportion'd and absurd.

The Idea.

Which being again vex'd with some hate and spite
That doth in them vengeance and rage excite,
Seem to be tortur'd and deformed quite

While so being fixt, they yet in them contain
Another sort of ugliness and stain,
Being with old wrinkles interlin'd again.

Lastly, as if Nature ev'n did not know
What colour every sev'ral part should owe,
They look as if their Galls would overflow.

Fair is the Mark of Good, and Foul, of ill,
Although not so infallibly, but still
The proof depends most on the mind and will.

As Good yet rarely in the Foul is met,
So 'twould as little by its union get,
As a rich Jewel that were poorly set.

For since Good first did at the Fair begin,
Foul being but a punishment for sin,
Fair's the true outside to the Good within

In these the Supreme Pow'r then so doth guide
Nature's weak hand, as he doth add beside
All by which Creatures can be dignified,

The Idea.

While you in them see so exact a line,
That through each sev'ral parts a glimpse doth shine
Of their original and form divine.

Therefore the characters of fair and good
Are so set forth, and printed in their blood,
As each in other may be understood

That Beauty so accompanied with Grace,
And equally conspicuous in the face,
In a fair Woman's outside takes the place.

Thus while in her all rare perfection meets,
Each, as with Joy, its fellow beauty greets,
And varies so into a thousand sweets.

Or if some tempting thought do so assault
As doubtful she 'twixt two opinions halt,
A gentle blush corrects and mends the fault.

That so she still fairer, and better grows,
Without that thus she more to passion owes
Than what fresh colour on her cheeks bestows.

To which again her lips such helps can add
As both will chase all grievous thoughts and sad,
And give what else can make her good or glad.

The Idea.

As Statuaries, yet having fram'd in Clay
An hollow image, afterwards convey
The molten metal through each several way,

But when it once unto its place hath past,
And th'inward Statua perfectly is cast,
Do throw away the outward Clay at last

So when that form the Heavns at first decreed
Is finished within, Souls do not need
Their Bodies more, but would from them be freed.

For who still cover'd with their earth would lie?
Who would not shake their fetters off and fly,
And be at least, next to a Deity?

However then you be most lovely here,
Yet, when you from all Elements are clear,
You far more pure and glorious shall appear

Thus from above I doubt not to behold
Your second self renew'd in your own mold,
And rising thence fairer then can be told.

From whence ascending to the Elect and Blest
In your true Joys you will not find it least
That I in Heav'n shall know, and love you best.

The Idea.

For while I do your coming there attend,
I shall much time on your Idea spend,
And note how far you all others transcend

And thus, though you more than an angel be,
Since being here to Sin and Mischief free,
You will have rais'd your self to their degree,

That so, victorious over Death and Fate,
And happy in your everlasting state,
You shall triumphant enter Heaven gate.

Hasten not thither yet, for as you are
A Beauty upon Earth without compare,
You will shew best still where you are most rare.

Live all our lives then, If the picture can
Here entertain a loving absent Man,
Much more the Idea whence you first began.

PLATONICK LOVE

DISCONSOLATE and sad,
    So little hope of remedy I find
That when my matchless Mistress were inclin'd
To pity me, 'twould scarcely make me glad,
    The discomposing of so fair a mind
Being that which would to my Afflictions add

    For when she should repent,
This Act of Charity had made her part
With such a precious Jewel as her Heart,
Might she not grieve that e'er she did relent?
    And then were it fit I felt the smart
Until I grew the greatest penitent

    Nor were't a good excuse,
When she pleas'd to call for her Heart again,
To tell her of my suffering and pain,
Since that I should her Clemency abuse,
    While she did see what wrong she did sustain,
In giving what she justly might refuse

Platonick Love.

Vex'd thus with me at laſt,
When from her kind reſtraint ſhe now were gone,
And I left to the Manacles alone,
Should I not on another Rock be caſt?
Since they who have not yet content, do moan
Far leſs than they whoſe hope thereof is paſt?

Beſides I would deſerve,
And not live poorly on the alms of Love,
Or claim a favour did not ſingly move
From my regard: if ſhe her joys reſerve
Unto ſome other, ſhe at length ſhould prove,
Rather than beg her pity I would ſtarve.

Let her then be ſerene,
Alike exempt from pity and from hate,
Let her ſtill keep her dignity and ſtate,
Yet from her glories ſomething I ſhall glean,
For when ſhe doth them everywhere dilate
A beam or two to me muſt intervene

And this ſhall me ſuſtain,
For though due merit I cannot expreſs,
Yet ſhe ſhall know none ever lov'd for leſs
Or eaſier reward. Let her remain
Still great and good, and from her Happineſs
My chief contentment I will entertain

Platonick Love.

Restrained hopes, though you dare not aspire
To fly an even pitch with my desire,
Yet fall no lower, and at least take heed
That you no way unto despair proceed,
Since in what form so'er you keep entire
I shall the less all other comforts need.

I know how much presumption did transcend,
When that affection could at most pretend
To be believ'd, would needs yet higher soar
And love a Beauty which I should adore,
Though yet therein I had no other end,
But to assure that none could love her more.

Only may she not think her beauty less
That on low objects it doth still express
An equal force, while it doth rule all hearts
Alike in the remot'st as nearest parts,
Since if it did at any distance cease
It wanted of that pow'r it should impart

Small earthly lights but to some space extend,
And then unto the dim and dark do tend,
And common heat doth at some length so stop
That it cannot so much as warm one drop,
While light and heat that doth from Heav'n descend
Warms the low Valley more than the Mountain top.

Platonick Love.

Nor do they always best of the Heav'ns deserve,
Who gaze on't most, but they who do reserve
Themselves to know it, since not all that will
Climb up into a Steeple or a Hill
So well its pow'r and influence observe,
As they who study and remark it still.

Would she then in full glory on me shine,
An Image of that Light which is divine,
I then should see more clear, while she did draw
Me upwards, and the vapors twixt us awe.
To open her eyes, were to open mine,
And teach her wonders which I never saw.

Nor would there thus be any cause to fear,
That while her pow'r attractive drew me near,
The odds betwixt us would the lesser show,
Since the most common Understandings know
That inequalities still most appear,
When brought together and composed so.

As there is nothing yet doth so excell,
But there is found, if not its parallel,
Yet something so conform, as though far least
May yet obtain therein an Interest,
Why may not faith and truth then join so well
As they may suit her rare perfections best?

Platonick Love.

Then, hope, sustain thy self, though thou art hid
Thou livest still, and must till she forbid;
For when she would my vows and love reject,
They would a Being in themselves project,
Since infinites as they, yet never did,
Nor could conclude without some good effect.

A MEDITATION

UPON HIS WAX-CANDLE BURNING OUT.

WHILE thy ambitious flame doth strive for height,
    Yet burneth down as clogged with the weight
      Of earthly parts, to which thou art combin'd,
Thou still dost grow more short of thy desire,
And dost in vain unto that place aspire
      To which thy native powers seem inclin'd.

Yet when at last thou com'st to be dissolv'd,
And to thy proper principles resolv'd,
      And all that made thee now is discompos'd,
Though all thy terrestrial part in ashes lies,
Thy more sublime to higher Regions flies,
      The rest being to the middle ways expos'd.

And while thou doest thy self each where disperse
Some parts of thee make up this Universe,
      Others a kind of dignity obtain,
Since thy pure Wax, in its own flame consum'd,
Volumes of incense sends, in which perfum'd
      Thy smoak mounts where thy fire could not attain.

A Meditation.

More more our Souls then, when they go from hence,
And back unto the Elements difpenfe,
   All that built up our frail and earthly frame
Shall through each pore and paffage make their breach,
Till they with all their faculties do reach
   Unto that place from whence at firft they came

Nor need they fear thus to be thought unkind
To thofe poor Carcafes they leave behind,
   Since being in unequal parts commix'd
Each in his Element their place will get,
And who thought Elements unhappy yet
   As long as they were in their ftations fix'd?

Or if they fally forth, is there not light
And heat in fome, and fpirit prone to fight?
   Keep they not in Earth and Air the field?
Befides, have they not pow'r to generate
When more than Meteors they Stars* create,
   Which while they laft, fcarce to the brighteft yield?

That fo in them we more than once may live,
While thefe materials which here did give
   Our bodies effence, and are moft of ufe,
Quick'ned again by the world's common foul,
Which in it felf and in each part is whole,
   Can various forms in divers kinds produce.

---

* In the Conftellation of Caffiopeia, 1572.

A Meditation.

If, then, at worst, this our condition be
When to themselves the Elements are free,
   And each doth to its proper place revert,
What may we not hope from our part divine
Which can this dross of Elements refine
   And them unto a better state assert?

Or if as clods upon this earthly stage,
Which represents nothing but change or age,
   Our souls would all their burdens here divest,
They singly may that glorious state acquire,
Which fills alone their infinite desire
   To be of perfect happiness possest.

And therefore I who do not live and move
By outward sense so much as faith and love,
   Which is not in inferior Creatures found,
May unto some immortal state pretend,
Since by these wings I thither may ascend
   Where faithful loving Souls with joys are crown'd.

OCTOBER 14, 1664.

ENRAGING Griefs, though you moſt divers be,
    In your firſt cauſes you may yet agree
To take an equal ſhare within my heart,
Since, if each grief ſtrive for the greateſt part,
You needs muſt vex yourſelves as well as me.

For your own ſakes and mine then make an end
In vain you do about a Heart contend,
Which, though it ſeem in greatneſs to dilate,
Is but a tumor, which in this its ſtate
The choiceſt remedies would but offend.

Then ſtorm't at once. I neither feel conſtraint,
Scorning your worſt, nor ſuffer any taint,
Dying by multitudes, though if you ſtrive,
I fear my heart may thus be kept alive,
Until it under its own burden faint.

October 14, 1664.

What is't not done? Why then my God, I find,
Would have me use you to reform my mind,
Since through his help I may from you extract
An essence pure, so spriteful and compact
As it will be from grosser parts refin'd.

Which being again converted by his grace
To godly sorrow, I may both efface
Those sins first caus'd you, and together have
Your pow'r to kill turn'd to a pow'r to save,
And bring my Soul to its desired place.

IN STATUAM LIGNEAM OVERBURII.

CERNIS Overburi, non ære aut marmore, vultum
  Sed Ligno Hiberno dic, age, nonne placet?

DE C. DE S

HÆC anima, ut fuerit terrenâ libera mole,
  Venerit et summo conspicienda Deo,
Talibus et tantis vitiis spurcata, trahetur,
  Haud dubium, ad pœnam suppliciumque grave.
Viderit: at pulchrum dabitur cum sumere corpus,
  Eximium, credo, perdere nollet opus.

EPITAPHIUM IN ANAGRAMMA NOMINIS SUI,
REDDOR UT HERBÆ.

QUAS turgens flos mane decet, quas aruit omnes
    Una dies, quas morte cita, nova vita sequetur,
Non unquam moritura tamen, sic *Reddor ut Herbæ.*

EPITAPH.
IN SE ROMÆ FACTUM 1615.

VEROS ceu varios populi ridere timores
    Expertus, vitæ melioris conscius, intus
Plaudebam, expectans faceret dum fabula finem.

IN TUMULUM DOMINI FRANCISCI VERE

ANGUSTUS nimis est lapis pusillus,
　　Vel, totum, foret ipsa terra, marmor ;
Angusta et spolia et Trophæa ficta,
Hæc Belgæ tulerant, vel illa Iberi
Cuncta angusta nimis videntur illi,
Qui victor toties mori volebat,
In se post alios, agens triumphum,
Ut dignum tumulum, Trophæa digna
Uni nil poterit referre vero.
Ni forte, ut maneat perenne nomen
Cui mundus spolia, et caro triumphus,
Cælum sit Tumulus, Trophœa stellæ.

IN DIEM NATALITIUM,
VIZ. 3 MAR.

VERE novo lux ufque redit quâ nafcor, at una
  Dum tempus redit, et fit numerofa dies,
Ver olim vires renovans, roburque recondens
  Ætas fit tandem, triftis hyemfque mihi.

FOR A DIAL.

DISCURRENS dubiæ, placidus compendia vitæ,
  Excipiens tacito gaudia tuta finu,
Præteritis lætare bonis, nec fæva futuri
  Exagitet miferos cura premave dies.

Omnis in adverfum ruit hora, volatque retrorfum
  Et velut exhorrens jam peritura fugit.
Dum numerans delet, dumque addens fubtrahit, illa,
  Quæ vitæ ratio, calculus atque tuæ.

IN ANSWER TO THE VERSES OF GUIET
FOR THE PUCELLE D'ORLEANS, QUASI EXTEMPORE.

QUOD nequiere viri, potuit si fœmina, quid ni
    Galle, fores tandem tu muliere minor?
Desine, Galle, tuam tandem jactare Bubulcam,
    Seu Medæa fuit, sive Medusa fuit.
Si canit ad Bellum, tamen est Medæa vocanda,
    Carmina dum rauco concinit illa sono
Hostes si cæsi, tamen est dicenda Medusa,
    Dum nimis ad diræ virginis ora rigent.
Virgo fit tandem sed qualem nollet adulter,
    Seu Medæa fuit, sive Medusa fuit.
Desinat ergo suam Gallus jactare *Johannam*,
    Saltem plena suo non erit illa Deo
Plena suo vel nulla datur, vel Papa *Johanna*,
    Numine, fit virgo quam licet illa minus

IN ANSWER TO TILENUS
WHEN I HAD THAT FATAL DEFLUXION IN MY HAND

QUÎ possim Phœbum succensum credere?
    Laudes
Quum facit ut scribas, Docte Tilene, meas.
Providus atque manum consulto surripit istam
    Ut melius possem nunc superesse tuâ

DE HUGONE GROTIO,
ARCÂ INCLUSO ET A CARCERE LIBERATO.

CARCERE dum Carcer victus, Tenebrisque Tenebræ
    Vinclis cum demum vincla soluta tibi
Prosiliens mediâ tandem de mole, videris
    Quidquid mortale est, deposuisse simul.

PRO LAUREATO POETA

AT quorsum Juvenis, si nullo limine clausus,
 Immistus canibus, saltuque vagatus in omni
Præcipites crebris damas latratibus urgens
Excurrit, secumque nihil non perdere tentat?
An mage grata viri tandem maturior ætas?
Qui furiis agitatus, atrox, atque omine tristi
Horrida funestis meditatur prælia campis?
In propriam speciemque ruens ita sanguine gaudet
Confessus satis, ut nullus sibi concidat hostis.
Is potiorne domi qui futilis ambit honorem,
Inque leves populi gyros proclivis et auram,
Mercatur voces, falsâque cupidine tractus,
Incertam dubii sectatur nominis umbram?
Heu fugias qui te fugiunt, et ferre recusant
Imperium fascesque tuos, quibus undique faustis
Candida supremos designant colla triumphos.
Sed ne nulla tibi demum victoria constet,
En prædam, formosa, tuam, quam porrigit herba,
Et genua amplectens, sese ultro dedere victam
Testatur, lauroque suâ tua tempora cingit.

Pro Laureato Poeta.

Nec canos caufere meos (qui fymbola certa
Sunt fidei), tantâ folitum flammâve tremorem,
Immo nec errones tanquam, fed lumina fixa
Contemplare oculos tandem, neque bafia fpernas
Floridus ut defit color ori, fervat odorem,
Æmula paftillis fpirabunt labra rofatis
Bafia, mellito et fe lingua madore refolvet.
Denique feu noftro latitet nova pruna colore,
Nictet et implexus torvo fub lumine cautus
Arcitenens, mortis tandem feu fcena futuræ
Prodierim, vitam nobis dum dura negaris ;
Ah! reddas faltem, nondum fatis arfit Amorem,
Cui fenium tempusve fidem cui præripit ullum.

AD SERENISS. REGEM GUSTAVUM,
AD 1631

PER varios terræ tractus & diffita Regna,
 Inclyte Suedorum princeps, dum caftra movere
Conftituis, pacemque pio decernere bello,
Quæ te fecurum probitas, prudentia fortem,
Felicem virtus præftat, non omine vano
Fecit, ut antiquum Germania libera nomen
Accipiens rurfus fe jufto vindice tandem
Gaudeat, inque tuos fuccedat fponte triumphos.
Scilicet hoc potuit tua dextera fortis & ultrix,
Igneus atque vigor bello famiatus, & enfis
Quo ftricto late rutilanteque, fulgidus hoftes
Irruis in medios, denfam paffimque caternam
Difcutis, & longe percellis quæque timore,
Ut tibi nec fumi nubes glomerata, nec imo
Excuffus pulvis, pila nec confertior inftans
Obfcurare tuos validos, vel flectere, greffus
Poffint, è multo quin numine flamma corufcans
Perftringenfque oculos, infultus reddat inanes

Ad Sereniss. Regem Gustavum

Militis, innocuosque ictus, ac irrita tela,
Dum tibi lustratæ cæcæ patuere tenebræ,
Inque tuam lucem caligo cedere visa est.
Inde citata tuum sequitur victoria cursum,
Inque gradus hæret certos figitque trophæa,
Auspiciisque tuis illustrior explicat alas,
Queîs sursum vecto, superas invisere sedes,
Inque novum tandem liceat tibi sidus abire
Clarius Arcturi, et fuscæ jubar addere luci.

EURYALE MŒRENS.

Depressæ valles piceis irriguæ fontibus,
    Herbæ marcidæ, cæca prætexentes **Barathra**,
Maligni colles hirfutis vepribus obfiti,
Afpera montium juga, exefis hiulca fpecubus,
Defrugatarum fegetum late patentia æquora,
Invifa Soli antra, confragofa præcipitia,
Abruptarum cautium nutantia undique cacumina,
Pendulæ taxi, cupreffis fuccrefcentes feralibus,
Spelæorum inferna ducentium horrores facri,
Infauftæ ftryges, bubulantia ftygiæ avis omina,
Rauci ftridores, torvorum colla anguium fibila,
Prodigialium monftrorum exerta paffim capita,
Afpectus truces fiderum, diri portenta ætheris,
Vofque gementes umbræ, hic teftari liceat,
Nihil ufpiam fuiffe Euryale triftius.

1632

MENSA LUSORIA;
OR, *A SHOVEL-BOARD-TABLE TO MR MASTER.**

ROBORIS excelsi tabulatum sternitur ingens,
   Æquore productum levi, quod tramite recto
Procurrens, tandem quâ se subducit in imum
Dissecat exilis transversim linea, scena
Unde patet ludi, commisso margine clausa,
Qui bini ternive notam certantibus aptat
Figitur extremo, seu pressus limite jactus,
Seu tremulus nutat, sibi nec constare videtur.
Hic ubi conveniunt lusores, quisque monetam
Argento cusam, disci formâque nitentem
Librat in adversam, quâ ducitur orbita, partem
Perpetuo jactu, sed quæ, si forte feratur
Plus justo, cadit in foveam, quæ limine summo
Cernitur, at citra septum si tarda satiscit,
Rejicitur jactus, totus sit & irritus inde.
Ast intra justam datur ut consistere metam
Promovet hic jactum, promotum dimovet ille.
Adjicit hic alium, sed quem depellere tentát
Nonnullus; Nummos hic obsidet, impetit ille,
Obliquo Cursu: Multà cadit iste ruinâ,
Dum complexa suo funduntur singula nexu,
Et variata vices rerum sors undique versat.
Ludere sic liceat manibus, sic ludere musâ,
A studiis fessi quum jam decessimus ambo.

---

* Thomas Master, "esteemed," says Anthony Wood, "as a vast scholar, a general artist and linguist, a noted poet, and a most florid preacher," was a senior student of Christ Church. He assisted Herbert in collecting materials for the *History of Henry VIII*. He died in 1643.

CHARISSIMO, DOCTISSIMO, JUCUNDISSIMOQUE JUXTIM AMICO THOMÆ MASTER.

Hoc Epitaph. mœrens P. C E B. Herbert de Cherbury, 1643.

QUI sis vel fueras, Amate Master,
    Lectorem satis hæc docere possunt,—
Quod terris fuit ut molesta vita,
Te dempto, mage sit molesta longe,
Quod Cœlum fuit ut beata sedes,
Auctum te, mage sit beata sedes.
In terris quid agis fide vacillans?
Si vita probus es, fruere, Lector,
Cœlo jam solito beatiore,
Master jam reliquis alacriore
Vivat in æternum virtus ac diffita terræ
Lustret, ubique gravi sub Religione resurgens.